SOMERSET'S COAST
a living landscape

Written and photographed by

NIGEL PHILLIPS

Natural Time Out
Publications

For Janet, Jessica and Alistair, the best of people to share a beach adventure with.

First published 2011

British Library-in-Publication Data
A catalogue record for this book is available from the British Library

ISBN 978-0-9557620-2-4

Published by Natural Time Out Publications, Somerset, England

Designed by Peter Creed, Oxford, England

Photographs by Nigel Phillips

Maps by Heard's Design

Printed by 1010 Printing International Limited, China

Cover photographs
Main picture: Sanderings *Calidris alba*, Dunster Beach
Small pictures (left to right): Nesting Fulmar *Fulmarus glacialis*, Glenthorne;
Painted Lady *Vanessa cardui*, Porlock shingle bank;
White Rock-rose *Helianthemum apenninum*, Brean Down

Contents

Foreword

Somerset has a wonderfully diverse coast and a very wide range of wildlife. The aim of this book is to paint a picture of these and highlight some of the species that most of us can see without necessarily being experts. It also examines how this wildlife uses the coast and explores some of the underlying principles of how these coastal habitats work.

Coasts have always been places of change. Over thousands of years the power of the sea has eroded many beaches and created new ones, again and again. The big difference now is that we have defined our beaches and coastal areas very tightly. Our sea walls and built environment of roads, housing, shops and holiday facilities are now squeezed-in right up behind the beach.

Before these built environments existed coastal habitats and their species achieved a balance. If the sea washed higher up the beach the dunes formed further back. Now, however, they are unable to do this because we are in the way. Such 'coastal squeeze' is a modern affliction affecting not only Somerset's coast but many other coastal areas across the UK and around the world.

Sea levels are rising due to the melting of the icecaps. This is a consequence of climate change which is a large and complicated topic not covered by this book. However, even small rises in sea level of just two or three millimetres a year are causing seas to reach higher up the beach. This leads to erosion of many types of coastal habitat including cliffs, saltmarshes, sand dunes and shingle banks.

There are no simple answers to these problems, but if we want to keep our coastal habitats we will have to do something about it. It is no good trying to hide our heads in the sand because there may be none left if we do not act. Ultimately, the aim of this book is to show what we have to lose.

Acknowledgements

I would like give a big thank you to those that helped to make this book happen.

Bob Corns of Natural England at Taunton for reading and commenting on the Landscape and Geology section. And for saying that a book on Somerset's coast would be a worthwhile thing to produce.

John Crothers for spending time talking about molluscs and providing me with a copy of *The Intertidal Invertebrate Fauna of The Severn Estuary*, Boyden, Crothers, Little and Mettam, a Field Studies Publication. A very long out of print, but immensely useful, booklet for someone trying to work out what lives where along the Somerset coast.

Professor Juliet Brody Natural History Museum London and Dr Nigel Chaffey Bath Spa University for providing their very up to date information on the distribution of seaweeds on the Somerset coast. In particular I would like to thank Juliet Brody for reading the section on seaweeds and for making some very constructive suggestions for improving the text.

Caroline Barrett for editing and proof reading the draft text and making it a much more readable book.

Janet Phillips for reading the draft chapters at a very early stage and pointing out where my sentences where half a page long.

And Peter Creed for his skill in designing the book and coping with me sending him far too many photographs to have to make a selection from.

Nigel Phillips
August 2011

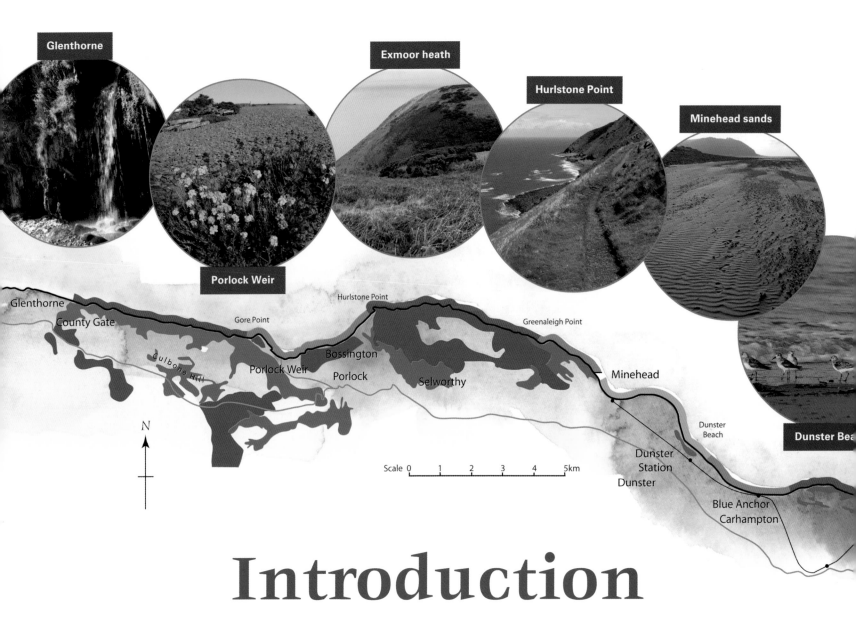

Glenthorne

Porlock Weir

Exmoor heath

Hurlstone Point

Minehead sands

Glenthorne
County Gate
Culbone Hill
Gore Point
Hurlstone Point
Porlock Weir
Bossington
Porlock
Selworthy
Greenaleigh Point
Minehead
Dunster Beach
Dunster Station
Dunster
Blue Anchor
Carhampton
Dunster Bea

N

Scale 0   1   2   3   4   5km

Introduction

When Somerset is mentioned it is often the rural interior of the county that dominates the imagination; orchards and cider; willows and withies; water-filled rhynes on the levels; sheep and cattle grazing in an intimately mixed landscape of grasslands and small woodlands with narrow lanes linking all together. The interior of Somerset is a wonderful place.

But Somerset also has a coast, with headlands and cliffs, shingle and sand beaches and river mouths. This coast is in fact one of the largest, most diverse, and most connected-up wild habitats that the county has left.

It has two well-known and dramatic landscapes standing sentinel at either end: in the west, Exmoor National Park, and in the east, the magnificent Brean Down. Somerset's coast links these two places both physically and ecologically. Oystercatchers, among many other coastal birds, are able to move from beaches at the foot of Brean Down to beaches lying at the foot of Exmoor without leaving their natural habitat, without even crossing a road, track or pavement.

Nowadays many of our wild places, particularly in southern Britain, occur only in small patches across a countryside that is busy with farming

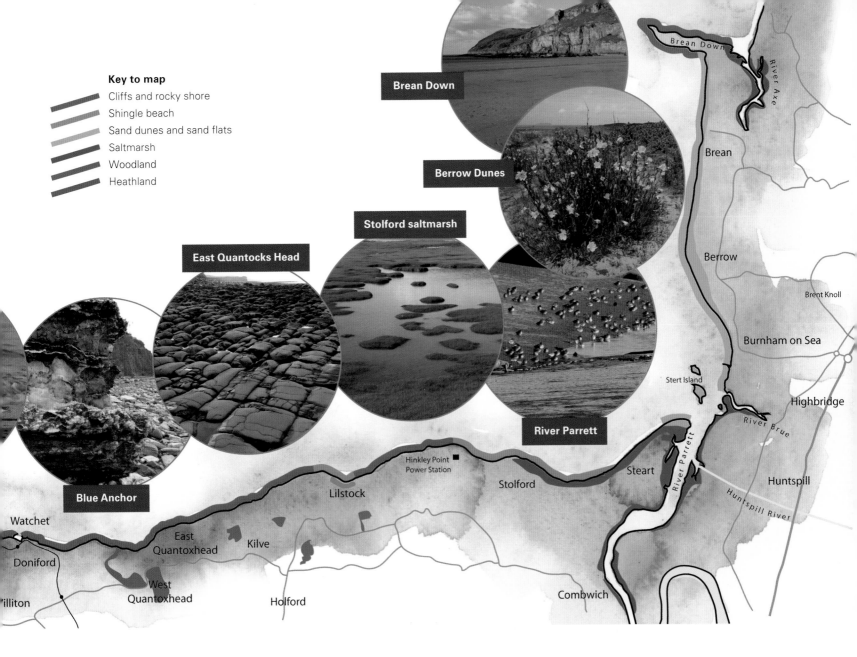

Brean Down

Berrow Dunes

Stolford saltmarsh

East Quantocks Head

River Parrett

Blue Anchor

Brean Down

River Axe

Brean

Berrow

Brent Knoll

Burnham on Sea

Stert Island

Highbridge

River Brue

Steart

River Parrett

Huntspill

Huntspill River

Hinkley Point
Power Station

Stolford

Lilstock

Combwich

Watchet

East
Quantoxhead

Kilve

West
Quantoxhead

Holford

Doniford

'illiton

activities and very much littered with our roads and housing. Somerset's beaches are still one gloriously long strip of connected-up, wild habitat; a 73 km long living landscape.

There is no escaping the fact that man's activities have had some impact on Somerset's coastline. Coastal defences, power generation and leisure developments have all taken a toll on its natural wonders, but much remains. This coast is still full of wildlife, both of plants and animals, and whatever the season, summer or winter, it is a captivating landscape with many surprises.

Looking beyond our own shores Somerset's coast is also hugely important to bird life, particularly waders and wildfowl, from countries in Europe and above the Arctic Circle. Many of these birds are dependent on this coast's rich intertidal feeding grounds to complete their migratory lifecycle.

The coastal area featured in this book matches the 'modern' Somerset County Council area. This runs from Glenthorne in the west to the River Axe in the east and is also the same area that the Somerset Wildlife Trust covers. The coastal habitats covered here include shallow sea, intertidal sand and mudflats, sand dunes and shingle banks, rock and boulder beaches, cliffs and cliff tops, and salt marshes.

1

Somerset's Sea

LEFT
From Brean Down, high tide over Brean and Berrow Sands,
Quantock Hills in the distance.

RIGHT, TOP TO BOTTOM
The sea's edge at Dunster Beach, a vital feeding area for waders.

Porlock Weir looking towards Gore Point.

Bridgwater Bay from Stolford, November rain.

Porlock Bay from Bossington Hill.

Shurton Bars, just west of Hinkley Point.

THE SEVERN SEA
one of the world's natural wonders

When you stand on the Somerset coast you are looking at both a sea and a river mouth. This is the Bristol Channel, often called the Severn Sea by Somerset residents, and also the mouth of the River Severn.

The whole of the Somerset coast is very much a marine environment with seaweed, sea fishes and sea shells found along its entire length. However, this coast also forms the southern shore of the vast mouth of the River Severn. The Severn is Britain's longest river at 354 km, just beating the Thames which is 346 km long.

With strong Atlantic Ocean swells pushing into the Bristol Channel Somerset's sea always tastes salty, but it is also an estuary where fresh river water mixes with the salty sea water.

Defining the point where a river becomes an estuary, and where an estuary finishes and becomes the open sea, is not always easy. The mouth of the River Seven is traditionally mapped at roughly the point between Weston-Super-Mare and Cardiff on the Welsh coast, 16 kilometres across the Bristol Channel. However, the sediments that turn the waters of the Severn estuary a pale coffee colour often extend as far west as Glenthorne on the Somerset county boundary. At this point it is roughly 27 km across the Channel to Porthcawl on the Welsh coast. Fairly soon after Glenthorne the sediment starts to disappear and the estuarine habitat becomes a true open-sea habitat.

The eastern part of the Somerset coast experiences the highest tidal range in the UK and the second highest tidal range in the world, with a 15-metre vertical height difference of sea level between the highest and lowest tides. (The highest tidal range in the world is found in the Bay of Fundy in Eastern Canada, with 17 metres between highest and lowest tides.)

At 24,500 hectares, the Severn estuary is one of the largest estuaries in the UK. The varied habitats of the estuary support many plant and animal species above and below water. Vast amounts of sand and mud—around 20,000 hectares—are uncovered at low tide making this one of the most important places in the UK for estuary birdlife.

Huge numbers of wildfowl and waders drop in to feed and rest here on their spring and autumn migrations. Some birds, such as Knot *Calidris canutus*, come to the Somerset coast as they travel between their summer breeding places in Siberia and their wintering grounds in West Africa. Others, such as Shelduck *Tadorna tadorna* will have travelled from various points in Northern Europe to spend the whole winter on the Somerset coast.

A 3,000-strong flock of wintering Dunlin *Calidris alpina*, many of which will have travelled here from their breeding grounds in Iceland, swooping and swerving over the sand flats at Steart in February, is ample evidence that this is a very important place for wildlife, both in the UK and in an international context.

A vital feeding place for many creatures

Over 100 species of fish have been recorded in the Severn Sea. For many of these, the mixing of seawater and freshwater is a critical element in providing the habitat and food they depend upon. The meeting of salt and fresh water on a massive scale, combined with huge tidal movements that churn the sand and mud flats, mixes plant and animal life into a protein-rich feeding ground. This has been taking place day after day, year after year, for around 5,000 years.

The ability of marine life to move freely into and across the Severn Sea is a critical factor in how this world-class estuarine ecosystem works. It is important for the many marine creatures that live below the surface and for other wildlife that depends upon this complex food chain. This includes the 70,000 wildfowl and waders that visit the Severn Sea coasts annually to feed during spring and autumn migration time.

This sea is not only important in its own right. The role it plays in feeding resident and migrating animals, below and above the water, inextricably links it to the well-

Somerset from Steep Holm, Brean Down to the left of picture, Brent Knowle to the right.

Lilstock bay on a very still May day.

Glenthorne beach, where the estuary becomes the open sea.

Selworthy Sands from Western Brockholes.

Dunster Beach, January frequented by many wildfowl and waders during the winter.

Greater Black-backed Gull
Larus marinus crossing
the mouth of the Parrett.

Black-headed Gulls
Larus ridibundus,
the most abundant gull
along this coast.

Shelduck *Tadorna
tadorna*, Dunster Beach,
up to 3,000 found along
the coast in winter.

Dunlin *Calidris alpina*
at Berrow, the Severn
Estuary is the most
important wintering ground
for these birds in Britain.

being of wildlife and ecosystems in many other parts of the world. These include Salmon *Salmo salar* which move out of the Severn Sea to the Faroe Islands and Norway; eels that travel from Somerset to breed in the Sargasso Sea; and wading birds such as Whimbrel *Numenius phaeopus* that stop to feed on Somerset's coast twice a year as they travel between their breeding grounds in Iceland and West Africa where they spend the winter.

Impeding the natural flow and mixing that takes place here between the rivers and the sea would be a very big and potentially dangerous step into the unknown. A proposal to build a 'Severn Barrage', a 16-km, tidal power-generating dam stretching from Somerset to South Wales has recently, and fortunately, been shelved by the UK government. Although it is desirable to replace fossil fuels with renewable energy, such a project, by altering the ecology of this huge sea and freshwater ecosystem, could have devastating effects on its ability to shelter and feed the many hundreds of species and many millions of individual animals that depend upon it. Perhaps a less damaging way to harness the power of this mighty estuary will be found in the future.

The Somerset coast is not a well-known place for seeing sea mammals but searching through the records shows a considerable amount of evidence of their presence in the area. It is likely that an increase in watching the sea

specifically for sea mammals from cliffs and headlands would show more activity than we are currently aware of.

The Atlantic or Grey Seal *Halichoerus grypus* occurs regularly on the shingle beach at the eastern end of Steep Holm, with up to eight having been seen at one time there. Records for Atlantic Seals at or close to Steep Holm go back to at least the 1970's.

Atlantic Seals are also periodically spotted just off the coast at Porlock Weir.

In June 2011 an Atlantic Seal had to be rescued from the Hinkley Point B nuclear power station after it got trapped in a water cooling chamber that is part of the system that takes sea water into and out of the power station.

Unfortunately most of the records for Dolphins and Porpoise are for stranded animals, either dead or dying. At least eight Common Dolphins *Delphinus delphis* have been found stranded

between 1993 and the current time. They have been found on several beaches including Brean, Minehead and Watchet. The Harbour Porpoise *Phocoena phocoena* has been recorded even more often with at least fourteen animals being found stranded between 1991 and the current time. They have been found on several beaches between Minehead and Burnham.

To partly offset the all the above stranded animals it is good to be able to report that a Harbour Porpoise was seen alive and swimming at Portishead in June 2011. Portishead is a considerable way up the Severn Estuary and only just below the Avonmouth dock area.

Fisherman going out on boats from Watchet and Porlock also report sightings of Dolphin and Porpoise. This would seem to be an area of Somerset's marine life that needs considerably more investigation.

Atlantic or Grey Seal *Halichoerus grypus*, found in Somerset's sea but not easy to spot.

Somerset's Coast

2

Landform and Geology

LEFT
Triassic rocks Blue Anchor,
one of the South West's most dramatic cliff landscapes.

RIGHT, TOP TO BOTTOM
Pleistocene cliffs at Donniford.

Blue Lias pavement, East Quantocks Head.

Minehead sands.

Ammonite *Psiloceras planorbis* fossils, Blue Anchor.

Part of the Porlock shingle bank.

Visiting the Somerset coast is like flicking through the pages of a beautifully illustrated field guide to geology and landform. There are so many sites with easy access and so many types of cliff face, rock, stratum and coastal formation, all close together.

It is the great geological diversity of the Somerset coast that creates a foundation for the surprisingly wide range of landscape types and habitats within them along this short coastline. Put in context, Somerset has 73 km of coast while neighbouring Devon has around 270 km between its north and south coasts, and Cornwall roughly 565 km.

The varied geology includes dunes and shifting shingle, vast areas of mud and silt exposed at low tide, limestone pavement beaches and low, perennially crumbling cliffs formed from soft mudstones and shales.

Somerset also has dramatic, high and rugged cliffs on its coastal county boundaries; sandstone at the Exmoor end and Brean Down's limestone at the other.

You will find layer upon layer of diverse rock, laid down in a wide range of climatic periods covering many millions of years.

The oldest coastal formations are the rocks that can be seen, and touched, along the Minehead to Glenthorne cliffs at the far western end of the coast. These are from the Devonian Period, 417–354 million years ago. The youngest coastal formations are the sands at Berrow at the opposite, northern end of the coast, which are still being deposited today.

A substantial proportion of the cliffs between Watchet and Hinkley Point are formed from Jurassic Blue Lias rocks. These cliffs are a northern extension of the same Jurassic strata that has been designated a World Heritage Site at Lyme Regis in Dorset. Although far less well-known than the Dorset cliffs, a similar range of fossils has been found eroding from these Somerset cliffs.

Only very brief details of some of the fossils that might be seen are included in the following geological descriptions. Further information on how to find out more about fossils that might be found here is included in the appendices.

Some 26 km of the Somerset coast, across several different sites, have been designated as Geological Sites of Special Scientific Interest by the UK government. Information on where to find further details on the geology of Somerset's coast is also included in the appendices.

CLIFFS, ROCKS AND FOSSILS

Reading the cliff face

Understanding the geology of Somerset's cliffs can sometimes be rather hard. The Earth's crust has shifted over millions of years, and many layers of rock visible in the cliff faces have been folded and squashed a great number of times by immense pressure deep underground before taking the positions they hold today. In some cases, due to a layer of rock sliding under another, younger rocks sit underneath older rocks. This confounds the usual view that the oldest rocks are to be found at the base of the cliffs and the youngest formations at the top.

As a result, some caution is required in interpreting Somerset's cliffs. Nevertheless, they remain fascinating places to visit. They have a kaleidoscopic array of rock types and fossils almost everywhere you look and they provide a stunning and stimulating backdrop to all the wildlife to be found on or around them.

The following descriptions of Somerset's cliffs give a broad picture of their formation and point out some of the highlights. For in-depth information there are a number of very good, detailed geological guides to almost all the county's cliffs which are listed in the Bibliography.

Starting in the far west

Some of the highest and most dramatic cliffs are found at Glenthorne. This is the most westerly point of Somerset's coast, where Somerset finishes and Devon begins. Rock material that is actively eroding from these cliffs eventually contributes to the shingle banks at Porlock and to other shingle banks further east along the Somerset coast.

Devonian Red Sandstone cliffs at Glenthorne
408 to 360 million years old, laid down horizontally but now twisted vertically by movement of the Earth's crust.

Old Red Sandstone cliffs at Glenthorne, the oldest rocks on Somerset's coast, the waterfall marks the boundary between Somerset and Devon.

Shingle beach and ridge at Stolford, the beach landscape here is continuously altered by the tides.

Burnham, Berrow and Brean Sands, one of longest continuous sand beaches in England.

The cliffs here are made up of the oldest rock formations found along the Somerset coast. These rocks are sedimentary and are known as Old Red Sandstone on account of the deposition of sandy sediments rich in iron oxides which give many of the cliffs their red colouration. The sediments were laid down during the Devonian Period (417–354 million years ago). Rocks from this period are the underlying solid geology of much of Exmoor and the Quantocks.

During the Devonian Period in Britain, this particular part of Somerset was part of a large continental landmass that included Europe and North America and lay south of the Equator. The Old Red Sandstone rock derives from sediments that originated during hot and very dry desert conditions interspersed with warm tropical seas.

FOSSILS YOU MIGHT FIND

The tropical seas provided the right conditions for some of the earliest forms of coral reef to thrive. These now fossilised reefs appear as thin bands of lighter coloured limestone within the Old Red Sandstone. The earliest forms of fish lived in these tropical seas and their fossils can sometimes be found. However, their great age and the enormous pressures put on them during movement of the Earth's crust mean that most of these fish fossils are squashed beyond recognition or broken. Some of the commonest fossils found in these cliff rocks are known as 'trace fossils'. This is where the rocks, once mud on a sea floor, show the fossilised marks or trails where marine worms or crustaceans burrowed through the marine sediments.

At the other end

Somerset's northern coastal boundary is marked by another remarkable landscape feature, Brean Down. Rising dramatically above the flat sand beaches that lie to the north and south of it, Brean Down marks the county boundary between Somerset and Avon. There are breathtaking views from its highest point which rises up close to 100 metres. Somerset's western boundary at Glenthorne is easily seen from here, as is the Welsh coast on the other side of the Bristol Channel, and if conditions are right, the Brecon Beacons which lie 65 km away.

Brean Down is formed from the second oldest type of rock found along the Somerset coast—Carboniferous Limestone, which started life in the Carboniferous Period (354–290 million years ago). Brean Down is the westerly extension of the Mendip Hills and both are created from the same Carboniferous Limestone. These pale-grey to dark-grey limestone rocks are derived from calcium-carbonate-rich mud deposited beneath an ancient sea.

During the period that followed the last ice age, and which ended approximately 12,000 years ago, melting glacier water caused sea levels to rise around the UK and Brean Down became an island. Slowly, over several thousand years, sand, silts and mud carried by the sea built up on the landward side of the island and joined it to the mainland again, as we see it today.

Five kilometres out at sea, Steep Holm is another

The island of Steep Holm seen from Berrow Sands.

extension of the Mendip Hills and is formed from the same Carboniferous Limestone rock. Although once all connected together, over millions of years Brean Down and Steep Holm have become separated from the main Mendip Hills by the eroding action of the sea and rain on softer parts of the rock.

On the southern side of Brean Down the zigzag pedestrian steps leading to the top of the Down cross what appears to be a steep, sandy cliff. This is in fact a far younger geological formation which dates from around 50,000 years ago when the region was made up of Arctic tundra-type habitat. This sandy, stony, deposit was blown by the wind or washed here by icy river waters and contains the bones of arctic foxes, reindeer, bison and lemmings—all animals that thrive under Arctic conditions. These are known as Pliestocene Deposits.

FOSSILS YOU MIGHT FIND

The Carboniferous Limestone rocks of Brean Down hold the fossil remains of some of the earliest marine life that flourished on this very old sea bed. They include crinoids, or sea-lilies, which are in fact animals and not plants, and several different types of coral.

Jurassic cliffs at East Quantocks Head. The bands of hard Blue Lias limestone rock in these cliffs are interspersed with softer shales and mudstones.

Cliff falls at Gore Point contribute new material that will eventually become smooth rounded stones.

Brean Down a dramatic landscape feature marking the northern extent of Somerset's beaches.

Brean Down cliffs, Carboniferous Limestone 360–280 million years old.

◄ **Donniford**, some of the youngest cliffs on Somerset's coast and made from sediments deposited during the Pleistocene 2 million–10,000 years ago.

◄ **East Quantocks Head**, Jurassic 200–150 million years old, fossil sea floor.

◄ **Blue Anchor Bay**, red Triassic cliffs 250–200 million years old, on the right, merge with the younger 200-150 million year old grey Jurassic cliffs.

Pink Gypsum from cliffs at Blue Anchor, also known as Alabaster and derived from sea water that seeped into ancient sediments during the Triassic period 250–200 million years ago. ►

The lower cliffs

Somerset's longest continuous coastal cliff landscape lies between Blue Anchor Bay and Hinkley Point. These cliffs run almost continuously for around 20 km and although lower than the cliffs found at Brean and Glenthorne they are spectacular landforms, rich in geological history. They are one of the best places in Somerset to see and find marine fossils.

The cliffs are formed from a succession of shales and limestones from the Triassic (250–200 million years ago) and Jurassic (200–150 million years ago) Periods which appear as a complex layering of rocks on the exposed cliff face.

The dominating features along this stretch of cliff coastline are the Lower Jurassic, Blue Lias 'pavements' that can cover considerable areas of the beach in front of the cliffs. These mostly smooth, undulating, grey, rock platforms are fossilised sea floors from very ancient seas. They are well-known for the large numbers of fossil Ammonites that can be seen in them.

More recent cliffs

At Donniford there is a section of cliff that is much younger, and made of softer material, than the cliffs lying on either side.

These are sediments, mainly gravels, that were deposited in a river valley during the Pleistocene Period (2 million–10,000 years ago). They are known as alluvial, or river, sediments and were deposited during Arctic-type weather conditions. Remains of the teeth and tusks of Arctic tundra-dwelling mammoths have been found in these sediments and give an indication of what the climate was like when this material was washed here.

Unlike most of the cliff rocks along this coast which date from many millions of years ago, the material that forms these cliffs, and the animal remains found in them, are recent in geological terms. The mammoths that contributed their bones and teeth to the Donniford cliffs lived on or close to the Quantock Hills, in a landscape that would have looked very much like it does today, albeit much colder.

An alien landscape

The cliffs that lie immediately to the east of Blue Anchor Bay are perhaps the most visually dramatic of all those along the Somerset coast. The grey-blue Jurassic cliff formations are intimately squashed up against the older red Triassic deposits. The red Triassic deposits should be lying neatly beneath the Jurassic rocks but have been turned on their sides, folded and mixed by the movement of the Earth's crust.

Recent land-slips contribute to the chaotic nature of the cliffs here, and when you add the presence of the pink, orange and white Alabaster that occurs here and that now lie in huge, several ton, chunks on the beach the whole scene has an almost alien appearance.

The degree of exposure and ease of access to these ancient rocks found between Blue Anchor, Watchet and at St Audries, where the late Triassic period moves into the Jurassic, make this part of the Somerset coast of the highest international importance among geological sites across Europe.

FOSSILS YOU MIGHT FIND
Ammonites (like the 50 cm wide *Coroniceras* pictured) were among the most numerous creatures found in the seas at this stage of the development of life on Earth. As well as a range of different ammonite species, these rocks also hold large numbers of fossilised shells of small marine animals that once lived on or in this sea floor. The fossil remains of marine reptiles such as Ichthyosaurs have also been found.

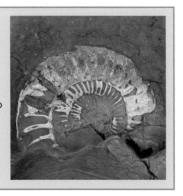

FOSSILS YOU MIGHT FIND
Of particular note east of Blue Anchor Bay is the appearance of the Ceratodus Bone Bed. This is a Triassic rock layer packed full of fish teeth and scales which takes its name from the substantial crushing teeth of the lung-fish *Ceradotus* that are found within it.

SHINGLE BANKS AND BEACHES

Most of the shingle found on the Somerset coast comes from the eroding cliffs that lie behind many of the beaches. Shingle is found along a large proportion of this coast but it disappears quite abruptly after the River Brue and northwards from Burnham. The degree of shingle found on the beaches, between high and low tides, can vary considerably from month to month and year to year. The rounded nature of the stones makes them easily rolled by wave and tidal movements and means that shingle on the lower part of the beach comes and goes. It can be readily pushed into new places or new shapes by the power of the sea. The movement of shingle along this coast is predominantly from west to east, and this is known as 'longshore drift'.

Porlock shingle ridge

The massive shingle ridge at Porlock was formed around 6,000 years ago. It is mainly made up of large amounts of rock and shingle deposited by much earlier glacial activity on coastal areas well west of Porlock. Rising sea levels started to erode this shingle and the sea's easterly longshore drift moved it into Porlock Bay over a relatively short period of time. Since that massive initial input of shingle, the amount of rock and stone contributed by more recent cliff falls has been very small. In fact, longshore drift has caused shingle to move away from this ridge towards the east, resulting in the ridge becoming progressively thinner since it was first formed. Currently, between Porlock Weir and Hurlstone Point, the Porlock shingle ridge stretches for just on 5 km.

Longshore drift continues to move shingle to the east and out of the bay and much of the small amount of new shingle that comes from cliff falls to the west are stopped from their natural easterly movement by heavy wooden groynes that have been constructed at Porlock Weir to help keep the entrance to the small harbour open.

This has all contributed to the gradual thinning of the shingle ridge. It eventually resulted in the sea making a substantial breach through the ridge during a storm in October 1996 and flooding the grazing marsh that lies behind it. Before 1996 heavy earth-moving machines had been used to reinforce the shingle ridge by pushing the shingle back into gaps caused by storm tides. However, a review of likely sea level rises in the future led to the realisation that this was a futile exercise and that the natural breaching process should be allowed to take place.

Shingle at Stolford and Steart

A shingle ridge, though less substantial than the Porlock one, has formed between Stolford and Steart. It once stretched right up to Hinkley Point but massive boulder sea-defences have reduced it considerably. Its current length is around 3.5 km. For about half its length, from Stolford to Wall Common, the ridge has little vegetation on it as it is regularly washed by higher tides. Heavy earth-moving machinery is still used periodically to maintain this part of the shingle bank as a sea defence to protect the land behind it from floods.

As at Porlock, in the light of possible rising sea levels, the cost of maintaining this shingle bank as a sea defence has been weighed against any cost benefits of protecting some of the agricultural land behind it, and it is likely that the sea will be allowed to breach it in the near future.

From Wall Common to Steart the shingle bank becomes progressively colonised and stabilised by vegetation and the shingle is mostly hidden.

Restoration of the shingle bank at Stolford following storm damage.

Stones at the east end of the Porlock shingle ridge, the seas action has graded the stones, carrying the smaller ones to the eastern end. This is known as longshore drift.

From Hurlstone Point the Porlock shingle ridge stretches for just over 5 km west to Porlock Weir.

The mixed large boulder and fine sand beach at Porlock Weir.

Stolford, the profile of the shingle bank here has been modified by heavy machinery to maintain it as a flood defence.

Dunster Beach, well vegetated sand dunes with a shingle bank and then fine sand on the lower shore, typical coast habitat between Blue Anchor and Minehead.

Berrow dunes, much of the landward sand dune habitat here has been lost to the highly invasive and planted Sea Buckthorn.

Looking west towards Minehead where the sand beaches give way to the high Exmoor cliffs.

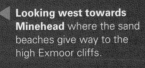

Berrow sands, despite new sand being continuously deposited by the sea, rising sea levels cause the waves to break higher up the beach eroding the dunes and creating new sand 'cliffs'.

THE SAND BEACHES

Sand beaches are exposed at low tide to varying degrees along almost the entire Somerset coast. Starting in the west, low sand dunes are found above the high tide line between Minehead and Dunster Beach, but the creation and active management of the golf course on the landward side here does not allow for much natural dune movement.

From Dunster Beach to Blue Anchor there is also a low sand ridge mixed with varying amounts of shingle. Another narrow, low sand-dune area lies behind the shingle ridge along the Wall Common to Steart section of the coast, although much of this is well hidden by vegetation.

The most extensive area of sand dunes is the Burnham to Berrow and Brean section which extends for some 9 km. As at Minehead, a golf course occupies a substantial part of this dune system, precluding natural movement of the sand and a dune flora from thriving. At the Brean end of these sand dunes, coastal defences as well as holiday and residential developments have obliterated the dunes to a large degree.

Still being made

The sand beaches are the youngest geological formations on the coast with most beaches receiving varying amounts of new material each year. Much of the sand on these beaches comes from sediments that are carried down the River Severn. They also come from the sandstone cliffs as they erode, and other rocks and boulders that fall onto the beach. These are then rolled around and broken down by the movement of the sea through wave and tide action into very small particles.

Fragments of broken up sea shells also contribute, to a lesser extent, to the formation of these sands.

New sea defences and a lost beach

After the sea breached the old Minehead sea wall during storm conditions in the mid 1990s new sea defences were erected. However, the new sea walls and massive boulder groynes leading out into the sea that were designed to break the power of the waves caused changes to the currents and tidal flows in Minehead Bay. Eventually this led to most of the sand on the beach in the front of the town being washed away. This left a much less bucket-and-spade-friendly, stone-and-boulder beach, and consequently some 300,000 tonnes of sand were trucked in to replace those lost sands.

THE AGE OF THE COAST

Around 12,000 years ago, the sea shore and the beaches and cliffs along the Somerset coast would have been around eight kilometres to the north of their current position and obviously much closer to what we now call Wales. This was due to vast amounts of water in the Northern Hemisphere being locked up in the glaciers that sat north of Somerset at this time. This caused the sea level to be about 40 metres lower than it is today.

As the glaciers melted sea levels slowly rose eventually flooding across the land to the point where we find the coast today.

The sea is still eating into the Somerset coast, with the harder rocks being eroded by less than a millimetre a year, but with some of the softer cliff faces disappearing at a rate of up to a metre a year.

3

Sea Life

Low tide at Gore Point with Devonian red sandstone rocks.

Shanny *Lipophrys pholis* rock pool, Gore Point.
Commonly found on beaches with boulders and rocks.

Common Coral Weed *Corallina officinalis*, Gore Point.
With the tiny 1 mm white spiral tubes of the tube worm *Spirobis corallinae*.

Common Brittlestar *Ophiothrix fragilis*, Gore Point.

Barnacles *Elminius modestus*, Gore Point.
Nine species of Barnacle have been recorded along this coast.

Green Shore Crab *Carcinus maenas*, Blue Anchor.
This is the commonest crab, dead or alive, that you will find along this coast.

UNDER THE WATER
The sublittoral zone—the area below the lowest tide

"Out of sight out of mind" was probably never more true than for the silt-laden, muddy-coloured waters of the Severn Sea. From the surface it looks as if nothing much is living out there, but this is very deceptive. These waters team with marine life. Sprats *Spratus spratus*, Skate *Raja batis*, Conger eels *Conger conger*, several species of prawn and shrimp, marine worms, marine molluscs and crabs are just a few of the many hundreds of species living in these waters.

Much of the silt in the Bristol Channel is held in almost permanent suspension. This is in part due to the constant input of silty water flowing down from the River Severn and its tributaries, and also to the movement of sea tides up and down the Bristol Channel. The sea off the Somerset coast is never still enough for much of the silt, sand and mud to settle on the sea floor. During the time of the highest tides, known as spring tides, up to 10 million tons of silt will be moving up and down the Severn estuary at any given time.

The large amounts of silt and other debris held in suspension in the Severn estuary are in fact the main key to its importance as a home for marine life. Vast quantities of tiny, edible fragments of animal and plant material come down the River Severn and its tributaries and mix with marine plankton brought in by the sea currents.

This mixture of silt, bacteria, microscopic animals and plants creates a nutrient-rich feeding ground for literally billions of slightly bigger, but still very small marine creatures, which are then in turn eaten by marine worms, shellfish and other fish, both large and small.

The Severn estuary is, in fact, a vast fish nursery. Ten species of fish that are of economic importance use these waters at different times in their life cycle, either for breeding or for feeding. Herring *Clupea harengus*, Cod *Gadus morhua*, Plaice *Pleuronectes platessa*, Sole *Solea solea*, Whiting *Merlangius merlangus*, Blue Whiting *Micromesistius poutassou*, Hake *Merluccius merluccius*, Horse Mackerel *Trachus trachus*, Ling *Molva molva* and Saith *Pollachius virens* all occur off the Somerset coast. Many of these fish will be caught later, out in the open seas by commercial fishing boats, when they have left the food-rich, sheltered and shallow Somerset waters.

Somerset's sea also plays a critical role in providing a home to fish that live in the sea for only a part of their lives, moving on into the upper reaches of rivers to breed and spawn in fresh water. These are the Atlantic Salmon *Salmo salar*, Sea Trout *Salmo trutta trutta*, Allis Shad *Alosa alosa*, Twaite Shad *Alosa fallax*, Sea Lamprey *Petromyzon marinus* and River Lamprey *Lampetra fluviatilis*.

All these species have suffered big declines in their populations in the last hundred years due to a variety of reasons which include pollution both in the sea and in rivers, overfishing and structures such as weirs impeding their progress upriver to breed.

The Allis and Twaite Shad not only share unfamiliar names but are both members of the Herring family and grow to between 30 and 50 cm in length. Both species are very particular about, and faithful to, their breeding rivers and also to the part of the sea into which they move and use for feeding. This has led, over many thousands of years, to the Severn Sea Allis Shad and Twaite Shad populations being genetically different from other populations of Shad in the UK.

A much better-known fish, at least by name if not by sight, which occurs off Somerset's coast is the Common Eel *Anguilla anguilla*. Common Eels spend most of their lives in fresh water where they feed but do not breed. The Somerset Levels, which lie behind a considerable portion of the coast, provide the perfect habitat for them. After some 10 to 20 years of freshwater life when they will have grown to between 80 and 120 cm, they head downstream into the Severn Sea and then out into the open ocean. They then undertake an epic journey of 4,000 km to the Sargasso Sea in the North Atlantic east of Cuba and Florida. Here the adult eels mate, spawn and die. Their young, known as elvers,

then take three or more years to make their way back to the Severn Sea and swim up rivers and streams to their chosen freshwater habitat.

Although our common eel populations have declined by around 90 per cent during the last 20 years, the Severn estuary remains the most important marine area in the UK for this species.

Fishing
In the past, the waters of the Severn Sea supported a substantial fishing industry along the Somerset coast. In the 1870s commercial fishing for Sprats and Herring took place at Minehead and Porlock and in 1910 there were three

▶ **Staked fishing nets at Stolford.** Adrian Sellick removing fish from the nets at low tide.

Fish in the Severn Estuary. ▶ Cod and Bass caught on lines from a Watchet charter boat.

Thornback Ray ▶ *Raja clavata*, Lilstock. Stranded by a fast falling tide in a rockpool.

commercial oyster *Ostrea edulis* dredging boats based at Porlock harvesting oysters.

Today sea fishing contributes relatively little to Somerset's economy although fishing with rods from the shore and from charter boats is a very popular activity along much of the coast.

One very ancient form of fishing using nets fixed to posts, and known to have taken place on the shores of the Severn Sea since the Bronze Age, still continues today. Lines of posts with wide-mouthed nets attached to them are erected on the beach at the lowest points to which the tide drops. During the time in which the tide flows

in, completely submerging these nets, and then flows back out again, there is a chance that a good number of fish will swim or be washed into the nets. Despite this appearing to be a very haphazard way to catch fish, it has proved over a long period of time to produce substantial and regular catches.

Currently there is just one commercial staked-net fishing business on the Somerset coast and this is at Stolford, although periodically other lines of staked nets are erected by local fisherman at places such as Watchet. These nets catch a wide range of fish including Mullet *Liza ramada*, Dab *Limanda limanda*, Plaice

Pleuronectes platessa, Skate *Dipturus batis* and Shrimps.

An impact on sea life

Few who visit the Somerset coast will be aware of the very large amounts of seawater used at Hinkley Point nuclear power station. Millions of cubic metres of seawater are continuously sucked in from pipes that extend out on the seabed and are used in the cooling systems of this electrical power generation plant.

Despite the use of mesh filters at the mouths of these suction pipes, huge quantities of tiny fish and other small marine creatures, as well as their eggs and larvae pass through the mesh and perish. In

addition, very large numbers of bigger fish also die as they are caught in the filter systems of the water inlet pipes.

Following its use in the power station, this seawater is returned to the open sea up to 10 degrees Centigrade hotter than when it was first sucked in. Although this might benefit some marine species others cannot tolerate such a sudden rise in sea temperature.

The impact that this water abstraction is having on Somerset's marine life, causing the death of such large numbers of fish and other aquatic life, is as yet very poorly understood. It can, however, only be having negative effects.

LIFE OF SHALLOW WATER
The intertidal zone—the area between the lowest and highest tide

Seaweeds

All the silt and mud that makes the Severn Sea such a good place to live for creatures like marine worms that burrow in it, can also make it a little hard for shallow sea life that needs exposure to good light levels to thrive. And seaweeds come into this category. Like land plants, all seaweeds need sunlight to photosynthesise to enable them to grow and thrive.

Despite the often very silty condition in this sea, seaweeds are found along the whole of the Somerset coast. They are exposed as the tides drop and are found growing on rocks or wooden breakwaters and are also found, often looking rather battered, mixed in with other sea debris on the tide line. Wherever seaweeds are found attached to a hard substrate they are not actually rooted into it they are just holding on, hence the use of the word 'holdfast' for the lower parts of these 'plants'.

Seaweeds are not classified as true plants because they lack an organised vascular system for absorbing nutrients through a root system. They are often referred to as macroalgae. They also differ from land plants in that many of them lack a robust stem or branches to hold themselves upright. Without the support of the sea they tend to flop.

At the base of a seaweed is where we find the holdfast which is used for attachment. From the holdfast arises a stem-like structure called a stipe and then comes the leaf-like part which is known as a frond or blade. Several species of seaweeds have gas-filled bladders in their fronds that help to keep the seaweed upright when underwater. The holdfast, stipe and frond all photosynthesise.

Some seaweeds such as Egg Wrack *Ascophyllum nodosum* may live for many years and grow longer each summer season. Others, such as Oar Weed *Laminaria digitata,* loose the bulk of their frond in the winter and grow a new one from their holdfast and stipe each spring. The holdfast and stipe may persist for up to 15 years in these bigger seaweeds.

Seaweeds are identified as three distinct types, as defined by their colours of red, green and brown. Traditionally it is stated that the green seaweeds are found on the higher shore, brown seaweeds on the middle shore and red seaweeds on the lower shore. However this has now been shown to be a too simplistic view. Whilst it is true that red seaweeds are better adapted to cope with lower light levels found in deeper waters, they may also be found high up on the shore, but shaded by large boulders, in caves or under the larger brown algae.

Around 725 species of seaweed are found around the UK. Recent survey work carried out by Professor Juliet Brodie of the Natural History Museum London and Nigel Chaffey of Bath Spa University has found the Somerset coast to have a considerably greater diversity of seaweeds than had been previously supposed. Around 100 species have now been recorded.

This new survey has found two species of green seaweeds, Silky Thread Weed *Derbesia tenuissima* and *Syncoryne reinkei* that are apparently scarce in the UK and also new records for Somerset. Also found was the red coralline algae Tufted Coral Weed *Corallina caespitosa*, this is not only a another new record for Somerset but also a recently discovered new species. Another species of note and newly found on Somerset's coast is the red seaweed, Branched Fern Weed *Osmundea ramossisima*. See Appendix 3 for a list of Somerset seaweeds.

There is a strong east to west gradation in seaweeds on the Somerset coast. Due to greater amounts of silt in the water at the eastern end , reducing the amount of light that can reach seaweeds, and the west to east reduction in salinity, the greatest variety of seaweeds are found at the western end of the coast. This is where the sea is at its most salty and the light levels in the water at their best.

You will find seaweeds along all of the Somerset coast but Lilstock has been shown to have a particularly good range of seaweeds uncovered at the lower tide levels. Watchet and

Bladder Wrack *Fucus vesiculosus*, **Blue Anchor.** These elongated bladders at the tips are the reproductive bodies.

Toothed Wrack *Fucus serratus*, **Blue Anchor.** Has no gas bladders to help it keep afloat.

Spiral Wrack *Fucus spiralis*, **Brean Down,** also known as Twisted Wrack.

Channelled Wrack *Pelvetica canaliculata*, **Brean Down.** The upturned edges on the fronds are very distinctive of this species.

Egg Wrack *Ascophyllum nodosum*, **Brean Down.** Each of the large egg shaped flotation bladders are produced annually.

◄ Gut Weed *Ulva intestinalis* and Tough Laver *Porphyra umbilicus*, Lilstock.

◄ Irish Moss or Carrageen *Chondrus crispus*, Gore Point.

◄ Oar Weed *Laminaria digitata*, Glenthorne. One of the largest and most distinctive seaweeds you will find on the beach.

◄ Wrack Siphon Weed *Polysiphonia lanosa*, Glenthorne. This red seaweed grows on stems of other seaweeds, usually Egg Wrack *Ascophyllum nodosum*, not on stones.

Tufted Coral Weed *Corallina caespitosa* and Sea Lettuce *Ulva lactuca*, Gore Point. ►

Blue Anchor Bay are also good places to look for seaweeds.

It is at the western end of the Somerset coast from Minehead towards Glenthorne where you will find the greatest number of seaweeds. Around 40 species can be found in this area with careful searching. This is also the place where you are most likely to find Oar Weed *Laminaria digitata* one of our largest brown seaweeds washed up on the beach. Oar Weed is a very robust and easy to identify seaweed. It grows up to two metres tall and is adapted to grow in the deeper water down to about six metres. The tide doesn't usually drop low enough to expose the areas where oarweed forms dense 'forests'. It is most often found on the shore after very rough seas have torn it loose from the seafloor. Oar Weed 'forests' provide a home for many fish and other marine animals like sea mats and small sponges. Oar Weed itself is also used as a place for other smaller seaweeds to attach themselves.

In fact all the seaweeds that occur along the Somerset coast whether big or small also carry out the vital function of providing a home, or habitat, for a wide range of the sealife of shallow waters.

Four robust brown seaweeds Egg Wrack, Toothed Wrack *Fucus serratus*, Bladder Wrack *Fucus vesiculosus* and Channelled Wrack *Pelvetia canaliculata* are some of the most obvious and larger seaweeds you will find regularly along this coast, with Egg and Bladder Wrack being the most widespread and abundant. All four of these will be found growing on rock strata, large boulders and old wooden breakwaters.

The green seaweeds can often be harder to identify than the brown seaweeds. A lot of them are very soft and silky making it hard to work out their shape and diagnostic features when they are left slumped and apparently shapeless at low tide. Around 18 green seaweeds can be found along the Somerset coast. Sea Lettuce *Ulva lactuca* is rather more robust than many of the other green macroalgae, keeping its shape well enough to be fairly confident of its identification features when you find it. The fronds of Sea Lettuce are not only of a similar size to our salad lettuce but have also been regularly eaten in the UK, more so in the past than now.

Many of the red seaweeds are similar to the greens in being rather shapeless without the support of the sea, and in consequence hard to identify when the tide leaves them stranded. There are however two sorts of red seaweed that do have very distinctive growth forms. One of these groups are the upright coralline algae which are very unlike what we traditionally think of as seaweeds. Coralline seaweeds may grow to around 10 cm and are hard and rather brittle. They were previously thought to be related in some way to corals. They have a rather stiff bushy structure due to the large amounts of magnesium and calcium carbonate in their cell walls which they have absorbed out of the sea water. When these seaweeds die and their holdfast breaks away from the rocks their hard white 'skeleton' becomes exposed and may survive for a considerable time as part of the tideline debris washed backwards and forwards by the sea. Two bushy coralline seaweeds are found along the Somerset coast. Common Coral Weed *Corallina officinalis* is generally the commoner. The newly discovered Tufted Coral Weed *Corallina caespitosa* has now been found on several beaches, one of these being Blue Anchor Bay.

The other red seaweeds that have a hard 'body' are the crustose coralline algae that form a pinkish mat on rock and boulder surfaces typically low down the shore. Like the upright coralline seaweeds these also have calcium carbonate in their cell walls which makes them fairly robust. Despite their well-defined and tough body these encrusting seaweeds are not easy to tell apart without the use of a microscope. Common Shore Paint Weed *Phymatolithon lenormandii*, one of several very similar Paint Weeds is commonly encountered and has a mauvish tinge.

The encrusting seaweed Common Shore Paint Weed *Phymatolithon lenormandii*, Gore Point.

Molluscs, seashells and other things

One of the greatest pleasures of a seashore walk is never knowing beforehand what you may see. The Somerset coast is linked by the sea to thousands of kilometres of other UK coastlines, as well as to oceans across the globe. Who knows what might be blown or washed up on its beaches.

Most things found washed up on the shore have had no choice in the matter. Empty seashells are in this category. It is only after their living occupants have died, most often having been eaten by a predator, that the empty shell will be carried by currents and waves up onto Somerset's beaches. Even though they are no longer alive these empty seashells continue to play a role in the life of the beach as they are eventually broken down into tiny fragments and become part of the beach sand.

The number and variety of shells found on the strandline is to a large degree a matter of chance dependent on waves and currents. Large numbers of shells can be washed onto the beach on one tide and then be pulled back into the sea on the next. Many shells end up in huge quantities in valleys and hollows on the seabed far out from the beach.

The fresh water coming down the River Severn into the estuary and diluting the seawater, causes a similar west-to-east reduction in diversity of marine molluscs as of seaweeds. Several species reach their eastern limit as they come into the Severn Sea, and

begin to reduce in abundance as they meet the Somerset coast. The Common Periwinkle, *Littorina littorea*, for example, which likes to feed on decaying seaweeds just about reaches as far as Brean Down and little further. The amount of sediment in this sea is not a problem for many marine molluscs because burrowing in mud is exactly what they like to do. It is the reduction in the salinity of the sea going east that does pose a problem for them.

The great habitat diversity along the Somerset coast, of sand and mud, rock platforms, boulders and shingle, encourages a wide range of marine molluscs to make these shores their home. They can be divided into two major groups: the bivalves which have two shells, as in Razor Shells and Cockles, and those with a single shell like Limpets and Whelks. There are also marine molluscs that appear to have no shell as it is much reduced or hidden inside them. These 'shell-less' molluscs include Sea Slugs, Cuttlefish and Octopus, all of which occur off the Somerset coast.

On the beaches that have cliffs, rocks and boulders, three types of marine animals are often abundant and hard to miss. They are Limpets, Periwinkles also known as Winkles, and Barnacles. Limpets and Periwinkles are single-shelled molluscs. Barnacles are crustaceans and very closely related to Crabs and Prawns. There are around 15 species of Barnacle around the UK and Western European shores and six of these are found on Somerset's coast.

All three of these types of 'sea shells' can sometimes be found in huge colonies numbering thousands of individuals in close proximity, and all three species have an uncanny ability to live where they are only submerged by the higher tides.

Limpets, Periwinkles and Barnacles succeed in living out of the sea for extended periods of time due to their water tight 'doors' which are very effective at keeping moisture in their shells while the tide is out.

Limpets pull themselves down incredibly tightly against their home rock and retain enough seawater in their shell to keep them going until their next wetting. They feed by grazing on the thin film of algae that covers lower shoreline rocks and the trails where their tongue or radula has rasped the algae from the rocks is often clearly marked. Periwinkles, too, feed on the thin algae mat covering the rocks but also graze on larger seaweeds. Barnacles feed by waving their modified legs through the hole at the top of their shells and catching small food particles that pass by once the tide has covered them up.

Molluscs that are found on these beaches include the Dog Whelk *Nucella lapillus* which is a predator of Barnacles, the Sting Winkle *Ocenebra erinacea*, a predator of many other molluscs which bores a hole in the shell of its prey, the Small Periwinkle *Melarhaphe neritoides*, Flat Periwinkle *Littorina obtusata* and Rough Periwinkle *Littorina saxatilis* which is the commonest

Rough Periwinkles *Littorina saxatilis* **and Barnacles** *Elminius modestus,* **Brean Down.** Barnacles are not seashells but are crustaceans and are closely related to crabs.

Flat Periwinkle *Littorina obtusata,* **Blue Anchor** found all along the coast, grazes on brown seaweeds.

Dog Whelk *Nucella lapillus,* **Lilstock.** This Whelk is feeding on the barnacles beneath it.

Sting Winkle *Ocenebra erinacea,* **Gore Point.** This mollusc gets its name from its habit of drilling a hole through other shells to feed on them.

Baltic Tellins *Macoma balthica,* **Berrow sands,** an important prey species for ducks and waders.

Painted Top Shell *Calliostoma zizyphinum,* **Gore Point.** The pointed shell and iridescent colours of this shell make it one of the easiest to identify. Hardly ever found east of Minehead.

Flat Top Shell *Gibbula umbilicus,* **Dunster Beach.** Also known as the Purple Top Shell. Kilve is about as far east as you will find it along the coast.

Common Limpets *Patella vulgata,* **Blue Anchor.** These Limpets have used their shells to grind a circular depression in the rock so they can pull down tightly without any gaps around the shell edge.

Common Cuttlefish *Sepia officinalis* **'cuttle', Minehead.** A mollusc like the above shells but the 'shell' acts as a skeleton rather than a protective shell. Occasionally caught alive in nets at Stolford.

Lugworm 'casts', Berrow sand flats.

Periwinkle found on Somerset beaches.

The Painted Top Shell *Calliostoma zizyphinum* is not often found east of Minehead, but the Toothed or Thick Top Shell *Osilinus lineatus*, Grey Top Shell *Gibbula cineraria* and Flat Top Shell *Gibbula umbilicalis* all extend east as far as Kilve but disappear soon after that point.

Seven types of Limpet are found on these beaches. The commonest, the Common Limpet *Patella vulgata* is also the largest, sometimes reaching 60 mm in length. The smallest is the Blue-rayed Limpet *Helcion pellucidum* at 15 mm. This species lives almost entirely on the stipe and fronds of larger brown seaweeds on which it feeds. Common Limpets can live for up to 15 years and have well-established feeding territories over which they roam. They also grind a neat depression into their home rock, using their shell edge. This allows the shell to fit very tightly when required.

Despite seeming to be very simple creatures molluscs are a very adaptable and successful group of animals as proven by the vast numbers of them crowding the rocky shoreline on this coast.

Not all molluscs lead as sedentary a life as Periwinkles and Limpets. Some, such as Cuttlefish, cruise far out into the open ocean. White chalky cuttlebones are found quite often among tideline debris along the Somerset coast, and with greater frequency as you go west. They are most likely to be from the Common Cuttlefish *Sepia officianalis*, the commonest of the three

large Cuttlefish species to be found off our coasts. Cuttlebones are the inner support structure of cuttlefish. Instead of forming a protective shell on the outside of its body this mollusc uses the same calcareous material to form an internal structure.

Perhaps the most surprising molluscs found on the Somerset coast are Octopus. Unlike the Cuttlefish, they have no internal structure that washes up on the shore and reminds us that they are living off the coast. The Curled Octopus *Eledone cirrhosa* is smaller than the Common Octopus and has a maximum arm spread of about 70 cm. This species turns up fairly regularly in lobster pots, particularly at the Porlock end of the coast. The Common Octopus *Octopus vulgaris* has also been recorded.

Both Cuttlefish and Octopus are in the Cephalopod branch of the Mollusc family. Ammonites were also Cephalopods. These two species which make their homes off the shores here provide an immediate and living link with the Ammonites whose fossils can be found in many ancient rocks along this coast.

Marine worms

Hundreds of species of marine worm and millions of individual worms live in the extensive mud and sand habitats that occur off the Somerset coast. Despite these worms being just about the most abundant type of wildlife along the coast they are perhaps the most overlooked. They live very concealed lives

under the mud and sand, or in rock crevices.

The most obvious signs of them are 'worm casts' that cover large areas of sand and mud uncovered as the tide starts to drop. These 'casts' consist of material that has been excreted by Lugworms. Each 'cast' has a corresponding small depression lying around five to ten centimetres away. The Lugworm, which is usually between 10 and 25 cm long, lives in a U-shaped burrow just beneath the sand's surface. The depression is where the Lugworm has sucked seawater and mud down into its burrow and into its mouth. It then digests all the minute food particles in the muddy mixture and the 'cast' is the waste that is pumped out the other end.

Many other species of marine worm show no signs of their activity because they do not come to the surface. They glide perpetually through the sand and mud sucking water, mud and small food particles in at one end and ejecting waste material from the other.

Although most worms keep a very low profile, one species, the Honeycomb Worm *Sabellaria alveolata*, constructs vast 'reefs' at and just below the lowest level that the tide drops to. These are surely one of the best-kept secrets of the Somerset coast. They may not be 'coral' reefs but these reefs still swarm with life in the way that tropical reefs do.

Honeycomb Worms live in very extensive colonies and each worm builds a robust tube 3–4 cm long by cementing together large numbers of sand grains. As with reefs formed by

Honeycomb Worm *Sabellaria alveolata*, **Stolford.** Sometimes reaching 20 cm high and tens of metres across the 'reefs' that these colonial worms build provides a home for many smaller marine creatures.

Sand Mason Worm *Lanice conchilega*, **Dunster Beach.** Although only around 4–5 cm high, this is still a significant construction for such a small creature. Most commonly found west of Watchet.

Beadlet Anemone *Actinea equina*, **Doniford.** Animals with tentacles that are closely related to corals, but unlike corals they move around on their chosen beach. Found from Glenthorne up to Brean Down.

Common Brittlestar *Ophiothrix fragilis*, **Glenthorne.** Although looking very obvious here, brittlestars have the uncanny ability to disappear into the smallest cracks. Porlock Weir at low tide is a good place to look for them.

Rock pool at Gore Point. ▶

corals, Honeycomb Worms build on top of each other as earlier generations die away. The Somerset reefs may cover hundreds of square metres and stand up to 30 cm high in sheltered waters. Honeycomb Worms feed by using a ring of short tentacles around their mouths to catch food particles that are washed past.

The reef structures built by these worms create an immensely important habitat for many other small marine animals along this shore. The large variety of microhabitats created in these reefs are occupied by shrimps, young fish, many small crabs and a wide variety of other worms and molluscs. Honeycomb Worm reefs occur along much of the Somerset coast but as they can only be seen as the tide drops to its lowest levels they are often overlooked.

When looking for Honeycomb Worms care needs be taken not to get caught out by the tide suddenly starting to come back in. The very clinging and deep mud that is often exposed at low tide should also be avoided. The reefs built by Honeycomb Worms are fragile and easily damaged by stepping on them, so great care is necessary if they are found. Honeycomb Worms like to anchor themselves to rocky strata which limits the numbers of beaches on which they can be found. Blue Anchor Bay and to the east of it is a good place to look for them at low tide. Stolford is also good, but the mud there can be daunting.

In several other places along the Somerset coast another worm make its presence known by the structures it builds. This is the Sand Mason Worm *Lanice conchilega*. It tends to occur in colonies rather smaller than the Honeycomb Worm and although its individual sand-feeding tubes could not be described as a reef they are very distinctive complex structures to be made by a worm.

Sand Mason Worms can reach up to 30 cm in length but the bulk of their body lies hidden beneath the sand. They construct a tube from sand and shell particles four to six centimetres tall which is topped by a fan-like structure. This fan structure is in effect a net which collects small edible fragments of plants and animals which are then picked off by the sticky tentacles of the worm.

Sand Mason Worms are found on many of Somerset's sandy beaches but only at the lowest of tideline levels as they do not like being exposed for long periods. The extensive sand beach at Dunster Marsh is a good place to look for them and they occur on several other sandy beaches east towards Brean Down.

More marine life — rock pools and boulder shores

The dramatic, convoluted and fractured Jurassic Limestone rock platforms and pavements that form the beach on many parts of the coast westwards from Hinkley Point provide a myriad of nooks and crannies, as well as small caves and sheltered overhangs. Both above and below the lower tideline these are important places for marine life to hide away. Careful searching of well-shaded and damp crevices on the lower shore is likely to reveal the Beadlet Anemone *Actinia equina*. Only when found submerged in a pool of water will its tentacles be extended. Out of the water it appears as a shiny and slightly elongated red or brown blob, with the larger ones about the size of a hen's egg. Sea anemones are animals closely related to corals and they use their sticky, stinging tentacles to catch food including smaller shrimps and fish.

At the western end of the Somerset coast, closer to the open Atlantic, marine life becomes even more diverse. Searching the lower tide line and rock pools at Porlock Weir and then travelling west to the massive Old Red Sandstone boulders that form the lower shoreline at Gore Point will reveal a wide variety of marine animals.

Following the tide down to its lowest point allows you to see creatures in rock pools before there is time for them to scuttle for the cover of a rock crevice or patch of dense seaweed. Among many other creatures to be found here are Velvet Swimming Crabs *Necora puber*, Broad-clawed Porcelain Crabs *Porcellana platycheles*, several species of Hermit Crab, Snakelocks Anemones *Anemonia viridis* as well as Beadlet Anemones. Careful searching will also reveal Common Brittlestars *Ophiothrix fragilis* and occasionally, the not-so-common, Common Sun Star *Crossaster papposus*. The Shanny *Lipophrys pholis* is the

◄ **Broad-clawed Porcelain Crab** *Porcellana platycheles*, **Glenthorne.** A small crab 3–4cm across. Always well hidden, and usually under big stones. Only found from Minehead and west.

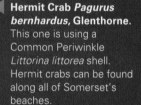

◄ **Velvet Swimming Crab** *Necora puber*, **Glenthorne.** The red eyes are a good diagnostic feature for this crab. Found from Hinkley Point and west.

◄ **Hermit Crab** *Pagurus bernhardus*, **Glenthorne.** This one is using a Common Periwinkle *Littorina littorea* shell. Hermit crabs can be found along all of Somerset's beaches.

◄ **Dead Spiny Spider Crab** *Maja squinado*, **Minehead.** This is a scarce crab along Somerset's coast and only likely to be found from Minehead and west.

Moon Jellyfish *Aurelia aurita*, **Porlock Weir.** ► Their sting can hardly be felt.

small shore fish most likely to be found in these pools.

Between Minehead and Glenthorne, a search of the sand, shingle and rocks that are exposed at the lowest spring tides can reveal other marine life that tends not to be found in the more regularly exposed, low-level rock pools. Great Pipefish *Syngathus acus*, Common Spider Crab *Maja squinado*, Edible Crab *Cancer pagurus*, Common Lobster *Homarus gammarus* and Edible Sea Urchin *Echinus esculentus* can all be found.

Occasional visitors

Some marine animals only make their way into very shallow waters for a brief, but important, part of their life cycle to breed. Many jellyfish come into this category. The Moon Jellyfish *Aurelia aurita* moves inshore during mid- to late summer, and the bay and harbour at Porlock Weir is a habitat that suits them well. This is a species that occurs from the southern edges of the Arctic Ocean down to the Equator and also into the Mediterranean. They spend most of their time out in the open sea feeding on a wide range of plankton and even small fish. But in late summer they gather together and travel in large swarms using the sun to navigate, into coastal waters and estuaries where they breed. Their tiny larvae, about one centimetre in length, then attach themselves to rocks or harbour timbers in sheltered places. The following spring, each of these larvae breaks into some 20 tiny jelly discs which then grow into new dinner-plate-sized Moon Jellyfish.

SOMERSET'S SUBMERGED FOREST

Submerged forest, Stolford.
Not boulders but the preserved trunks of ancient trees.

One of the most astonishing sights on Somerset's beaches are the preserved trunks and branches of trees that once formed a woodland around 4,500 years ago where the sea now washes. These trees on the beach were alive before the building of Stonehenge began.

At places such as Stolford, long dead Oak, Alder, Birch and Pine are slowly eroding out from the layers of peat in which they lie. These trees are not yet true fossils; they are still soft and woody.

As well as the trees there are extensive areas of preserved woodland-floor debris such as twigs and branches, all looking uncannily fresh when you consider how old they are. Essentially they were killed by a sudden inrush of sea water caused by a general rise in sea levels but there appear to have been periods of withdrawal by the sea that allowed more peat to develop over the fallen trees. They have been preserved by a combination of being buried in the peat and then

soaking in salt water which has inhibited the bacteria, fungi and insects that would normally cause the breakdown and decay of wood.

The presence of these trees and of the peat, as well as ancient pollen grains that have been found in the peat of species such as Common Reed, indicate that this very old woodland was similar to the Alder carr, or wet bog woodland, that is found on the Somerset Levels today.

Similar areas of preserved ancient forest can be found at low tide at Minehead and Porlock.

These 'submarine forests', as they are marked on Ordnance Survey maps, are graphic evidence of how sea levels rose when the glaciers melted at the end of the last Ice Age. Despite being of a similar age to Stonehenge these ancient relics from a past Neolithic landscape sit on Somerset's beaches for all to see and touch. They are, however, undoubtedly very special and should be treated with great respect.

4

Wildlife on the Beach

Painted Lady *Vanessa cardui*, **Porlock shingle bank**,
the landward side of the shingle bank has a mild microclimate and is a
popular spot for butterflies.

Shelduck *Tadorna tadorna*, **mouth of the River Parrett mudflats.**

Hare's-tail *Lagarus ovatus*, **Minehead Dunes.**

Oystercatcher *Haematopus ostralegus* **eggs, shingle bank,
Wall Common.**

Biting Stonecrop *Sedum acre*, **Dunster Beach.**

Six-spot Burnet moth *Zygaena filipendula* **on Meadow Vetchling**
Lathyrus pratensis, **Berrow dunes.**

Much of the diverse marine life of Somerset's coast lies hidden beneath the waves, but the animal and plant life of the beaches and upper shores can be very conspicuous.

During the summer months the cliff tops, dunes and shingle banks have extremely diverse, sometimes exotic, plant displays and many species of butterfly are associated with them. The summer and winter birdlife of the upper shores is equally varied and plentiful.

But there is no doubt that it is the extensive mud and sand flats, exposed when the tide goes out, that provide one of the most dramatic wildlife sights found on this coast. Vast numbers of waders and wildfowl come here during the winter months to escape the harsh north European and Arctic winter, making this one of the most important and spectacular places for winter shore birds in the UK.

BIRDS OF THE SAND AND MUDFLATS
The intertidal zone

Waders and wildfowl occur on Somerset's beaches throughout the year but only during the winter months do large numbers of birds move in from areas north and east of the UK.

From Brean Down west to Minehead, the entire 43-km sweep of sand and mud that is exposed at low tide provides rich feeding grounds for a wide range of shore birds that make this their regular wintering area.

The mouth of the River Parrett, lying between Burnham on Sea and Steart, also provides significant additional winter bird habitat along the coast, as do the much smaller rivers, the Axe and the Brue. The River Parrett is a major estuary feature within the vastly bigger Severn Estuary. In addition, sandy Steart Island and other shifting sandbanks that come and go in the mouth of the Parrett combine to create good feeding areas and safe roosting places for gulls, ducks and waders.

These glistening mudflats can be covered with thousands of birds. Up to 80,000 geese, ducks, waders and gulls can be found feeding across the Severn Estuary in the depths of winter. They feed on small crabs, marine worms, shellfish, fish and algae that are exposed as the tide rapidly drops away.

As well as being used by long-distance travellers like Wigeon *Anas penelope* from Russia and Dunlin *Calidris alpina* from Iceland, these mudflats are also feeding grounds for many local birds including Grey Heron *Ardea cinerea*, Little Egret *Egretta garzetta*, Canada Goose *Branta canadensis* and Mute Swan *Cygnus olor*.

The numbers of birds that come to the Somerset coast depend upon the severity of the weather elsewhere. Bridgwater Bay has its own regular site-faithful ducks and wading birds that fly in to the same beaches and mudflats year after year. But these regulars are joined by other winter visitors if the weather is harsh in the north and east of the UK. Birds that have travelled from northern Europe to winter on east coast sites such as the Wash in East Anglia, will move to Bridgwater Bay if temperatures drop well below normal winter levels or if snow sets in on the east coast. The winter climate on these south-west coastal beaches is usually considerably milder than on east coast beaches.

In addition, if inland freshwater areas on the Somerset Levels start to freeze, many hundreds of ducks including Shoveler *Anas clypeata* and Pintail *Anus acuta*, move to the coast to feed on the rich algae and microscopic invertebrate 'soup' found in shallow water at the tide's edge.

The importance of this coast to the bird life of Britain and Europe is recognised through a series of designations that have been given to it. The Bridgwater Bay Site of Special Scientific Interest (SSSI) forms the core area of these extensive sand and mudflats, covering 3,574 hectares, and runs from Brean Down to Lilstock. A major part of this SSSI also forms the Bridgwater Bay National Nature Reserve. An area larger than the SSSI has also been identified as important from a European perspective and is a Ramsar Site, a Special Protection Area (SPA) and a Special Area of Conservation (SAC). These European SPA and SAC designations have meant that the area has also been further designated as an Important European Marine Site (EMS).

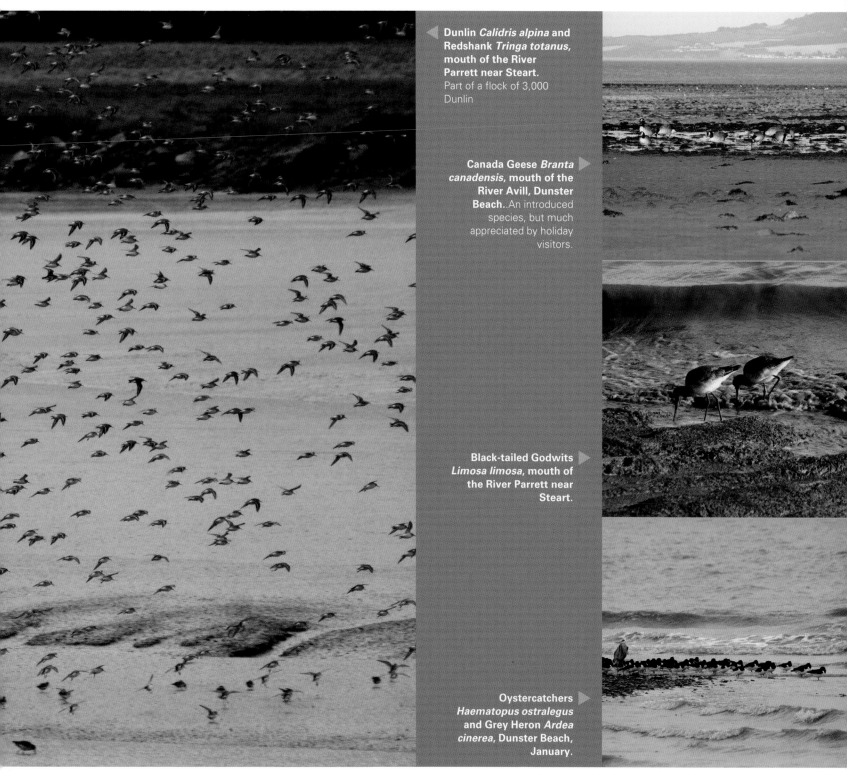

◄ **Dunlin** *Calidris alpina* **and Redshank** *Tringa totanus*, **mouth of the River Parrett near Steart.** Part of a flock of 3,000 Dunlin

Canada Geese *Branta canadensis*, **mouth of the River Avill, Dunster Beach.** .An introduced species, but much appreciated by holiday visitors. ►

Black-tailed Godwits *Limosa limosa*, **mouth of the River Parrett near Steart.** ►

Oystercatchers *Haematopus ostralegus* **and Grey Heron** *Ardea cinerea*, **Dunster Beach, January.** ►

Ducks

The most obvious members of the wildfowl or duck family to be seen on Somerset's beaches are Shelduck *Tadorna tadorna*. They often gather in groups of several hundred to feed in the shallows, and during the winter months are a beautiful and exotic presence along this coast.

They are large birds, almost the size of a goose. From a distance they appear black and white with a dash of orange and red. When lit by low winter sun their predominantly white plumage, orange chest band, glossy green head and crimson bill contrasts sharply with dark winter skies and muddy seas.

Shelduck most commonly feed just around the tide line in mud that is soft enough to allow them to sift through it for food items. They move their beaks rapidly from side to side through the silt picking out small marine snails and worms that form their favourite food. During late summer and into the winter months up to 4,000 Shelduck may be spread along the coast between Dunster Beach and Brean Down.

Most Shelduck found here will have travelled from where they have bred in other coastal areas of the UK and Ireland, with possibly a few coming from Europe. The majority of those which breed in Britain and mainland Europe go to the Waddensea on the west German coast in late summer where around 100,000 Shelduck gather to moult. However, since the 1950s Bridgwater Bay has provided an alternative safe place to feed and loiter while they shed their primary flying feathers and grow new ones. Bridgwater Bay is now the second largest moulting area for Shelduck in Europe.

Despite such large numbers coming to feed here only around ten pairs of Shelduck attempt to breed along the Somerset coast. They are hole-and-crevice nesting ducks and make use of places such as old rabbit burrows in well-vegetated sand dunes, as well as in hollows between boulders in cliff-fall areas. Breeding numbers are known to have been much higher along this coast before holiday developments and golf courses were constructed on several of the dune areas.

Numerically, Wigeon are the second most important duck after Shelduck to winter along the Somerset coast. Mainly occurring from the mouth of the River Parrett west to Dunster Marsh, their numbers peak around December and January when between 2,000 and 3,000 birds may be found along the coast. The biggest groups, of up to 200 or 300 birds together, mainly occur at the mouth of the River Parrett.

Wigeon often appear as rather dark ducks, sitting out on the sea in groups and keeping very close together while getting battered by heavy waves and spray. When sitting out at sea like this they are not feeding but waiting for the tide to drop and expose the macroalgae that they like to feed on. They favour Gut Weed *Ulva intestinalis*, a green, slimy seaweed, that is tubular and looks a little like intestines, and Sea Lettuce *Ulva lactuca*. When the tide is right up at the top of the beach Wigeon will often move to feed on vegetation on the saltmarsh just behind the beaches at Steart and Stolford. They will also move to other nearby fields behind the beach to feed on grasses and meadow plants, often choosing to visit at night when there is likely to be less disturbance.

Wigeon come to the Somerset coast from Iceland, Scandinavia and Russia with just a few hundred coming from northern parts of Britain where they breed during the summer months. Although the numbers seen along the coast may seem impressive they are dwarfed by the 16,000 or so Wigeon that winter at places like West Sedgemoor on the Somerset Levels during December, January and February.

Several other species of wildfowl visit this coast during the winter time, but in much smaller numbers than Wigeon. Teal *Anas crecca*, Mallard *Anas platyrhynchos*, Pintail and Shoveler are regularly seen out on the sea or feeding on the mudflats, as are small numbers of Brent Goose *Branta bernicula*.

Another winter-visiting duck is the Common Scoter *Melanitta nigra*. This is another bird that breeds mainly in Iceland and across to Siberia, with just a few pairs breeding in the north of Scotland and Ireland.

Common Scoters may sit several hundred metres out to sea, and their all-black plumage combined with a choppy sea can make them difficult to identify in poor winter light.

◄ **Shelduck** *Tadorna tadorna*, **Dunster Beach**, feeding at low tide, the males are larger with heavier red bills.

Teal *Anas crecca* **on the River Axe by Brean**, the smallest duck in Europe. ►

◄ **Wigeon** *Anas penelope*, **Dunster Beach**, they may have travelled here from Iceland or Russia.

Pintail *Anas acuta* **at Stolford**. A regular visitor during the winter months. ►

Waders

In addition to the ten or so species of wildfowl that regularly visit in the winter months, there are a number of wading birds for which this coast plays a vital role in helping to maintain UK and European populations by providing high-quality, winter-feeding grounds.

There are 13 migratory waders that occur regularly on Somerset's beaches in the autumn, winter and spring months: Oystercatcher *Haematopus ostralegus*, Ringed Plover *Charadrius hiaticula*, Golden Plover *Pluvialis apricaria*, Grey Plover *Pluvialis squatarola*, Lapwing *Vanellus vanellus*, Knot *Calidris canutus*, Sanderling *Calidris alba*, Dunlin *Calidris alpine*, Black-tailed Godwit *Limosa limosa*, Whimbrel *Numenius phaeopus*, Curlew *Numenius arquata*, Redshank *Tringa totanus* and Turnstone *Arenaria interpres*.

Other waders also occur but in smaller numbers, or only for a short time, before moving to other wintering grounds. In total at least 20 species of waders may be seen on the coast throughout the year.

The Curlew, though not the most abundant or the most distinctly plumaged wader to visit this coast, is probably the most noticeable due to its size. It is Europe's largest wader—a very big bird with a wingspan of between 80 and 100 cm. Its body size is in fact only a little smaller than a Herring Gull *Larus argentatus*, and it can often be mistaken for a gull when seen in flight.

Its long legs, large size and distinctive, heavy, down-curved bill make it unmistakable. The only similar birds likely to be on the same beaches are Whimbrel, which only occur in small numbers of 200 or so maximum, and as passage migrants, dropping in to feed briefly during spring and autumn migration periods before moving elsewhere. Whimbrel are smaller birds than Curlew with considerably shorter legs and bills.

No Curlew breed right on the coast but in the summer months around 40 pairs breed inland on the Somerset Levels.

From late summer and throughout the winter up to 2,000 can occur along the coast. They travel to Somerset, to find a milder winter climate, coming from the north of the UK and also from Norway and Sweden and further east. Curlew can be seen in every month of the year and on all the beaches between Glenthorne and Brean Down. Those that are present on beaches during the summer months are most likely to be first-year birds, those born in the previous year who will not breed until they are in their second year.

When out on the sand and mudflats, the Curlews' diet consists mainly of marine worms like Ragworm *Nereis* and Lugworm *Arenicola* which they catch by inserting their bills deep into the mud. They also pick food off the surface and take small molluscs and shore crabs from pools.

At the opposite end of the scale in size from Curlew is the Dunlin, which is a little smaller than a Starling *Sturnus vulgaris*. They may be small waders but the large numbers in which they occur give them a sizeable presence on Somerset's beaches. Between 10,000 and 15,000 Dunlin can be found here between October and February. The largest numbers are found on the coast at Stolford and Steart, around the mouth of the River Parrett and along the Burnham and Berrow sandflats.

In total around 500,000 Dunlin come from northern Scandinavia and Siberia to spend the winter in the UK and Ireland. The majority of those that breed in the uplands of the UK mainly migrate to West Africa during the winter, but some also come to the Somerset coast. The Severn Estuary holds around 10% of the British wintering population and is the single most important wintering ground for Dunlin in Britain.

Dunlin have bred in Somerset in the past on the high moorlands of Exmoor but the last records were back in the early 1900s. Their loss as a breeding bird is likely to be linked to the reduction of Exmoor moorland habitat which had been almost halved by the late 19th and early 20th centuries. This loss was caused by agricultural improvement of the wet moorland by draining and ploughing to create new grasslands for livestock grazing. Dunlin numbers are continuing to decline in Europe because of the same factors.

The biggest flocks of Dunlin on the Somerset coast, up to 3,000 together, occur on and over the mudflats at the mouth of the River Parrett and also back along the river as far as Combwich. When the rising tide pushes the Dunlin off the open coast mudflats, they move into the broad mouth of the Parrett. This can create a spectacular

◄ **Curlew *Numenius arquata*, Dunster Beach.** Around 2,000 Curlew may winter on Somerset's coast.

Female Curlew, Stolford, their bills are considerably longer than the males. This is Europe's largest wader. ▶

◄ **Dunlin *Calidris alpina*, Berrow sands**, a very productive feeding ground.

Dunlin, Combwich. When the tide is high Dunlin and other waders will be found feeding several kilometres up the River Parrett. ▶

scene as they wheel and land and then restlessly rise again in dense flocks. Different groups will be forced to join together as the incoming tide reduces the muddy river bank to a narrow strip and they are often accompanied by hundreds of Wigeon and Redshank.

The vast sandflats at Brean and Berrow that are exposed when the tide drops are another place where large numbers of Dunlin may congregate. These beaches are also the most reliable places to see Sanderling. As the tide drops and the food-rich sand flats are exposed, Sanderling will come in to feed. Rushing backwards and forwards at the sea's edge, they feed on small marine invertebrates that are still close to the surface of the mud and sand and that will burrow deeper as the sand dries out. Sanderling feed almost exclusively on the tideline and move around at a very fast pace. This combination of behaviours can be a helpful diagnostic feature.

Sanderling breed up in the high Arctic where the summer is short, and their chicks are often hatched by the second week of July. Following this very brief breeding period the adults start to move south again and in consequence several hundred adults can appear on Somerset beaches at the end of July. Some Sanderling may stay in the UK for the entire winter while for others the Somerset coast is just a staging post on their way to West and South Africa.

The best time to see Sanderling is in February and March when the beaches are very quiet and they are less

harried by human and canine beach visitors. Visitors who come to the beaches to watch Sanderling and other waders in the depths of winter should not forget that these birds may be very hungry and cold. They should be given space and allowed to feed undisturbed. Getting enough food at this time of the year really is a matter of life or death for them.

It is during the winter time that the sand dunes at Burnham, Berrow and Brean, and the vast areas of sand that are exposed at low tide, are at their wildest. With several thousand wintering birds coming into feed as the tide drops these beaches are well worth visiting.

Knot and Grey Plover are two waders with very similar colouring during the winter, both having simple grey plumage with few distinguishing features. Grey Plovers breed in Siberia and Knot in Greenland and northern parts of Canada. Both come to winter on Somerset's beaches between September and March.

Despite having similar plumage their behaviour and shape set them apart. Knot have relatively short legs for wading birds and often look rather plump and stubby. Up to 5,000 Knot occur along the coast, often in groups several hundred strong with Stolford, Steart and the mouth of the Parrett being their favourite places.

Grey Plover are longer-legged and stand more upright than Knot. They are also much less gregarious and are often seen as single birds among other wader flocks. Grey Plover only occur in small numbers along

this coast ,with often a maximum of 200 or 300 spread between Dunster Marsh and the Brean sandflats.

The Turnstone is another faithful winter visitor to these beaches and can be seen along almost all of the Somerset coast. Turnstones nest in rocky and stony habitats high above the Arctic Circle in places such as Greenland and Svalbard, and in consequence seem very much at home on Somerset's rockier beaches. Between 300 and 400 Turnstone visit them with the highest numbers usually present between August and December. Their name very much describes the way they feed, using their bills to turn stones over on the beach and then pounce on any unsuspecting marine life underneath, including small fish and crabs. Turnstones are also very adept at bulldozing heavy piles of seaweed in their hunt for small marine creatures to eat.

Research by the British Trust for Ornithology, involving ringing and recapture work, has shown that Turnstones can live for up to 22 years. This work has also shown that Turnstones are not unique in having such a long life span. Other coastal birds such as Grey Plovers, Greater Black-backed Gulls *Larus marinus* and Common Gulls *Larus canus* are all now known to live for at least 25 years.

Considering what rugged lives many of these coastal birds lead, being battered by winter storms, undertaking long migratory journeys and with some breeding in harsh Arctic environments, it is a tribute to their toughness that they live for so long.

Sanderling *Calidris alba*, **Dunster Beach, early August,** just arrived from their northern breeding grounds and not yet in winter plumage, also a Dunlin far right with black stomach and longer bill.

Grey Plover *Pluvialis squatarola*, mouth of the River Parrett.

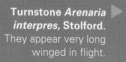

Turnstone *Arenaria interpres*, Stolford. They appear very long winged in flight.

It also highlights the huge responsibility that we have to ensure that large enough areas of high-quality wintering habitats like the Severn Estuary are retained.

Many migrating birds spend from autumn to spring on the Somerset coast. Many of them, we now know, may have been doing this for over 20 years. This is their home territory. They could not simply move elsewhere if these food-rich mudflats where to be reduced in size by offshore or shoreline developments. All the other good places to feed are already occupied by other long-standing and site-faithful groups of wintering birds.

The sand flats at the mouth of the River Parrett and the mudbanks of the river itself as far upstream as Combwich, are often covered with thousands of Dunlin, Redshank, Shelduck and gulls that have been pushed into the mouth of the river by the rising tide. Then, as the tide turns and recedes again almost all return to feed on the rich pickings of the newly exposed seashore.

The Avocet *Recurvirostra avosetta* is one winter-visiting wader, however, that sticks resolutely to the landward side of the mouth of the Parrett whether the tide is in or out. Avocets were first recorded as winter visitors in the Parrett estuary in 1939 and they have occurred regularly up to the present day. In the 1970s and 1980s the numbers recorded were in the range of between four and nine birds. They now number between 60 and 70 and can be found between August and February, with peak numbers usually in November

and December. Ringing of chicks from a strong East Anglian breeding population has shown that most of those birds winter in Spain, Portugal and north-west Africa. It is thought, therefore, that the River Parrett Avocets will have come mostly from breeding areas in mainland north west Europe.

During the winter the mudflats and low, sparsely vegetated islands at the mouth of the River Brue just south of Burnham also attract good numbers of waders. Redshank often feed here in loose flocks of between 30 and 40 birds alongside Ringed Plovers in similar numbers.

The mouth of the River Axe, immediately north of Brean Down, with Somerset's boundary running down the middle of the river, is equally attractive to Redshank and Ringed Plover. Both species can also be seen along the length of the Somerset coast, often mixing with other waders but often just two or three birds together, and, particularly in the case of Redshank, as single birds.

Both species remain to breed on the Somerset coast during the summer months, but finding nesting sites that are secluded and safe from disturbance caused by human summer visitors to the coast can be a problem for them. Between 1,500 and 2,000 Redshank occur along the coast as late-summer and winter visitors, but only a couple of pairs attempt to breed each year along the coast and nearly always on salt marsh areas behind the shingle banks. Around 40 pairs of Redshank breed on the Somerset Levels, across the West Sedgemoor, Catcott and Shapwick area.

The highest numbers of Ringed Plover are often seen in August and September when around 800 to 1,000 birds appear on the beaches between Dunster Beach and Brean. Some of these will be passage migrants who stop off on Somerset's beaches on their way from their breeding grounds in northern Europe to winter in southern Spain or north-west Africa. Many Ringed Plovers that breed in the UK stay here for the winter and a good number of these will winter on the Somerset coast. Up to ten pairs attempt to breed on the shingle beaches between Dunster Beach and Steart.

The Oystercatcher is a very conspicuous wader on Somerset's beaches throughout the year. Its black-and-white plumage and heavy, red bill make it virtually unmistakable. It occurs as a resident, a winter visitor and as a passage migrant. Between 500 and 1,000 wintering birds can be found along the coast, with many travelling down from Scotland and Iceland. During the summer around ten pairs of Oystercatchers attempt to nest along the coast, but as with Redshank and Ringed Plover it can be hard to find quiet, safe nesting sites during the summer months. Oystercatchers will nest on sand dunes, on shingle and also on rock outcrops. Despite being so versatile in their choice of nesting sites, and despite the fact that so much potential habitat is available, probably less than half of the ten or so pairs that attempt to breed each year manage to produce young due to disturbance by human and canine coast visitors.

◄ **Avocets** *Recurvirostris avosetta*, **at the mouth of the River Parrett near Steart**, much more wary than other waders found on this coast.

Redshank *Tringa totanus*, **Combwich**, breeds along the coast in very small numbers. ►

◄ **Oystercatchers** *Haematopus ostralegus*, **Berrow sands**, feeding on molluscs and marine worms.

Ringed Plover *Charadrius hiaticula*, **Stolford.** A breeding resident and winter visitor. ►

Herons

Little Egrets *Egretta garzetta* are not waders but herons. They are also supremely adept at wading about and feeding, in the shallow waters that cover the sand and mudflats as the tide comes and goes. They are now seen on Somerset's beaches throughout the year, but only 20 years ago they were a scarce visitor to the UK's wetlands. Their arrival as a resident breeding bird in Somerset follows a rapid expansion of their population northwards up through France in the 1970s. They now breed in the Somerset Levels with many of them travelling to the coast to feed, during the winter months. Highest numbers occur around November and December when around 40 to 50 Little Egrets can be found around the mouth of the River Parrett between Stolford and Burnham.

The Grey Heron is likely to turn up on almost any Somerset beach, but Stolford and Dunster Beach seem to be favourite places for them with up to 20 Herons being seen together at Dunster Beach during the winter.

Seagulls

Gulls can be found along the entire length of the Somerset coast. To many people they are the very essence of coastal wildlife; strong, agile flyers, at ease in gusting sea winds, and with beautiful plumage. To others they are rather scary, big birds that will lunge at unguarded picnic sandwiches.

It is deep in the nature of seagulls to scavenge and make the most of any food that might come their way. They are adept at spotting food scraps and

pieces of fish floating on the surface of the sea or at spending a lot of time and effort turning over tideline debris in the hunt for dead crabs, fish or anything vaguely edible.

Five species of gull occur regularly along the coast: Black-headed Gull *Larus ridibundus,* Common Gull *Larus canus,* Lesser Black-backed Gull *Larus fuscus,* Herring Gull *Larus argentatus,* and Greater Black-backed Gull *Larus marinus.*

The Black-headed Gull is regularly the most abundant of these on Somerset's beaches and in its harbours. Up to 4,000 birds can be present around the mouth of the River Parrett during the September to January period. None breed along the coast, but two to three pairs breed inland on the Somerset Levels.

Herring Gulls are the second commonest gull to occur, seen along all parts of the coast on rocks and sand with the highest numbers, some 400 to 500 together, occurring at the mouth of the Parrett. Around 400 pairs of Herring Gulls breed along the coast. Surprisingly, only around 20 pairs nest on natural cliff sites while the rest build their nests on ledges of buildings adjacent to the beach at Hinkley Point, Watchet and Minehead.

Lesser Black-backed Gulls have also taken to nesting on buildings with about 30 pairs sharing the same sites as Herring Gulls, and just a couple of pairs nesting on the westerly cliffs. Lesser Black-backed Gull numbers are boosted by winter visiting birds, some of which may come from Scandinavia.

Greater Black-backed Gulls sit at the top of the gull pecking order. Very substantial,

muscular birds, and bigger than Buzzards *Buteo buteo*, they will eat anything, alive or dead, that they can swallow. They are seen along the coast throughout the year but only in small numbers, with a maximum of 30 to 50 birds at any time, and with the highest numbers seen in late summer and into autumn. Two or three pairs breed irregularly on cliffs at the western end of the coast.

The Common Gull does not occur in large numbers on these beaches with only about 100 birds present at any time, and only as winter visitors arriving around September. Common Gulls breed on the west coast of Ireland, Scotland and in northern Europe. Birds on Somerset beaches are likely to be from any or all of these populations.

Cormorants

There are two well-known coastal birds that are, perhaps surprisingly, not that conspicuous along this coast. The least common is the Shag *Phalacrocorax aristotelis,* which is a very infrequent visitor to the Somerset coast from Devon cliffs to the west where it breeds. They are most likely to be seen at Hurlstone Point and to the west.

Cormorants *Phalacrocorax carbo,* are considerably more abundant than Shag, but still only 20 to 30 birds occur along the coast at any one time. They are seen regularly on sandbanks in the River Parrett estuary and on Steart Island, as well as at the mouths of the Rivers Brue and Axe. They breed inland on the Somerset Levels with around 20 pairs nesting colonially in trees.

Little Egret *Egretta garzetta*, **Stolford**, now a common sight along the coast but still exotic looking.

Common Gull *Larus canus*, **front left, Berrow beach**. In the background Lesser Black-backed *Larus fuscus* and young Greater Black- backed Gulls *Larus marinus*.

Herring Gull *Larus argentatus*, **Watchet**. Second commonest gull along the coast.

Cormorant *Phalacrocorax carbo*, **at the mouth of the River Brue.**

Lesser Black-backed Gull *Larus fuscus*, **Brean sands**, note the orange legs.

Greater Black-backed Gull *Larus marinus*, **Lilstock.** Somerset's largest and scarcest breeding gull.

SAND DUNES
The upper beach or supralittoral zone

It is no surprise that the parts of the Somerset coast man has coveted most for his own use are the sand dunes. Camp sites, caravan sites, hotels, cafes, houses and golf courses have all been built on or next to the Somerset sands. Burnham and Berrow, Dunster Beach and Minehead have all developed busy holiday businesses based on the sandy habitat that humans find so inviting.

Once, these sandy beaches were quiet, empty places, the haunt of large numbers of nesting birds. Gulls and waders nested commonly on the sand-and-shingle mix above the high-tide line. They have cryptically coloured eggs, matching sand and shingle, developed over millions of years to allow them to nest on the open beach. Their eggs were so well camouflaged they could escape detection by all but the most determined predators. Before the 1870s and the invention of the seaside holiday by the Victorians, these Somerset beaches were a nesting haven for such coastal birds.

Until modern esplanades and their roads as well as massive concrete-and-boulder sea defences were built, the Somerset coast had around 19 km of upper shore dunes. Although now somewhat reduced they are still found at Minehead, Dunster Beach, Burnham, Berrow and Brean. Steart Point also has a small area of upper-shore sand dunes and Steart Island is a sand-dune island.

Today, around 12 km of upper-shore, sand-dune habitat remains. Most of it is now confined to a very narrow strip, sometimes only a couple of metres wide, as at Minehead where the tightly mown golf-course greens sit hard up against the diverse dune flora. Six kilometres of Somerset's sandy coasts have been heavily modified with the creation of sea defences in the shape of concrete walls and massive boulder barriers made from non-local rock.

Burnham, Berrow and Brean

The 9 km beach that stretches from Burnham to Brean is one of the longest continuous sand beaches in the UK and Somerset's most dramatic wide-angle seascape. During the winter it is the haunt of migratory coastal birds, and in the summer months the dunes support a wonderful diversity of plant and animal life. This long, sandy beach also supports a considerable holiday industry which does have an impact on the range of wildlife that occurs here.

The dunes that lie immediately to the north of Burnham are rather poor in species. Not surprisingly, heavy summer trampling combined with housing developments right on the dunes has severely reduced the diversity of plant and animal life here.

Plants found in the dunes that lap against Burnham's

housing are more plants of dry, waste ground than a real dune flora and include Charlock *Sinapsis arvensis*, Field Bindweed *Convolvulus arvensis* and Common Dandelion *Taraxacum officinale*. The highly invasive Sea-buckthorn *Hippophae rhamnoides* also dominates many of the dunes here leaving little space for less robust species.

Fortunately, only a short distance north of Burnham the diversity of the dune wildlife increases significantly. At Berrow there is the largest remaining dune system on the Somerset coast. Here, 200 hectares of beach habitat has been designated as a Site of Special Scientific Interest and part of this area is also a Local Nature Reserve owned by Sedgemoor District Council. The coastal habitat at Berrow Dunes is one of the most botanically rich areas in Somerset with several hundred species of flowering plants finding a home here. These dunes also have a wide range of bird and insect life.

Even though the dunes are used by large numbers of holidaymakers, Berrow Dunes still have a great feeling of untamed wildness about them. The mobile nature of the dunes means they are never exactly the same from month to month and are often very different from year to year. The pioneering nature of many of the plants found here also means that you can never be sure of what you will find.

Sea-buckthorn *Hippophae rhamnoides*, **Minehead dunes**, the berries are an important winter food for birds.

Wild Mignonette *Reseda lutea* and **Fragrant Evening-primrose** *Oenothera stricta*, **Berrow Dunes**.

Berrow Dunes, although Sea-buckthorn *Hippophae rhamnoides* has dominated a major part of these dunes they still have a very diverse flora.

Honeysuckle *Lonicera periclymenum*, **Berrow Dunes**, a common climber on shrubs on the landward side of the dunes.

The first line of sand dunes above the high tideline are known as 'foredunes'. They are the front line of the dune system and are formed as high tideline debris slows wind-blown sand sufficiently to let it drop and start to accumulate. This fresh sand comes from lower down the beach where it has been deposited by the sea.

The freshly blown-in sand appears to be an inhospitable place to live but there are several plants which specialise in colonising this shifting and often very dry habitat. At Berrow Dunes Lyme Grass, *Leymus arenarius* is the first plant to colonise the mobile sand that has caught in the tideline debris. Lyme Grass is actually a fairly scarce coastal plant in the West Country. It is found at only a handful of sites in Somerset, between Minehead and Brean, and at only one site in Devon and one in Cornwall.

The sand starts to accumulate more quickly once Lyme Grass appears. Lyme Grass forms robust tussocks that are very effective at catching the blowing sand. The grass then grows taller rapidly in response to being swamped. Marram *Ammophila arenaria* is a similar grass, though shorter, and considerably more common across the UK. It also occurs on the dunes at Berrow. It usually gets a foothold behind Lyme Grass and carries out a similar role in stabilising the freshly accumulated sand. Once these pioneering grasses have started to carry out their work, other plants soon follow. Growing a few metres back from the unstable front line of the dunes, where the sand is a little firmer, plants such as Fragrant Evening-primrose *Oenothera stricta* and Sea Spurge *Euphorbia paralias* soon start to appear among the Marram grass tussocks.

The bright yellow flowers of Evening-primrose are a distinctive sight along many of Somerset's sand and shingle beaches. All species of Evening-primrose come from the Americas and were introduced into the UK as garden plants in the 1700s. The Fragrant Evening-primrose, very common at Brean, comes from Chile, while Common Evening-primrose *Oenothera biennis* and Large-flowered Evening-primrose *Oenothera glazioviana*, which are also both found at Brean Dunes, come from North America.

It is important to remember that these sand-dune habitats are not as static as many other habitats found further inland. The foredunes in particular are liable to move around, driven by the power of the wind and sea. During the summer months the dunes will creep towards the sea as dry sand is blown up the beach by offshore winds and accumulates as it catches on upper tideline debris. In the winter, strong winds, combined with stormy seas pushing high up onto the beach, can blast away the new foredunes created during the summer. This is the very nature of this dune habitat. Many plants that are found here, such as Sea Spurge, Sea Bindweed *Calystegia soldanella* and the grasses Sand Couch *Elytrigia juncea*, Marram and Lyme Grass are highly specialised, sandy-ground colonisers that occur only on new dunes and nowhere else.

The presence of old foredunes lying in parallel bands behind the current foredunes indicates that the creation of new dunes is a successful and regular process. It is known that the dunes in front of the Burnham and Berrow Golf Course have advanced roughly 100 metres towards the sea since 1945.

At Brean many of these older dunes have now become colonised by a dense scrub of Hawthorn *Crataegus monogyna*, Blackthorn *Prunus spinosa*, Sallow *Salix* sp., Elder *Sambucus nigra* and Sea-buckthorn.

Sea-buckthorn is a robust, sharply spined, thicket-forming coastal plant that occurs naturally on the east coast of England. It has been introduced on to many west coast dune areas as a way to help stabilise sand dunes. It was often planted around new beachside housing or holiday developments and their roads as a defence against the shifting dunes that would regularly inundate them. It was first planted at Burnham and Brean around 1890. This coincides with the opening of the Burnham and Berrow Golf Club on a substantial part of the dunes in 1891.

The older, well-vegetated dunes are known as fixed dunes and up until the early 1900s the grassland that developed on them was used by local farmers as grazing land for their cattle and sheep. It was this grazing that kept the shrubs and young trees we now see from gaining a foothold. Rabbits are now the

◄ **Fragrant Evening-primrose** *Oenothera stricta*, **Berrow Dunes**, one of three species of Evening-primrose found there.

Sea Spurge *Euphorbia paralias*, **Berrow Dunes**, now only found between Steart and Brean Down. ▶

Lyme Grass *Leymus arenarius*, **Berrow Dunes**, ▶ the pioneer plant that stabilises the new sand at the front of the dunes.

only large grazing animals found on the dunes and without them and their grazing much of the remaining flower-rich grassland would disappear under the advancing scrub.

Plants can be found in flower on these dunes from March to November, but May, June and July are the months to see the best of the rich flora that grows here. Visitors in these midsummer months will find Common Restharrow *Ononis repens,* Common Bird's-foot-trefoil *Lotus corniculatus,* Hare's-foot Clover *Trifolium arvense,* Lady's Bedstraw *Galium verum,* Salad Burnet *Sanguisorba minor,* Yellow Rattle *Rhinanthus minor,* Eyebright *Euphrasia nemorosa,* Pyramidal Orchid *Anacamptis pyramidalis* and Bee Orchid *Ophrys apifera* among many others.

The Lizard Orchid *Himantoglossum hircinum* is also found at Berrow Dunes and this is currently the only place where it is found in Somerset. It was first found here in the 1930s. During the time that they have been known at Berrow, Lizard Orchids have been found in two or three different areas. Currently there is just one colony of around 50 plants growing on the golf course.

The beautiful pink and white Sea Bindweed is also found here but now only in very small numbers, because unfortunately this plant seems to be declining at many of its traditional coastal sites in the UK. It used to be found at Minehead, Porlock and Stolford.

The tall pink-flowered Soapwort *Saponaria officinalis* is another garden escape that

grows happily on these dry dunes during midsummer. Originally from southern Europe its leaves produce a soapy lather when rubbed in water.

Many low-growing, dry-habitat grasses thrive on these dunes but Red Fescue *Festuca rubra* is by far the commonest. The Sand Sedge *Carex arenaria* is another dune specialist that only occurs here on Somerset's coast and not inland.

Sedgemoor District Council, Somerset Wildlife Trust and local conservation volunteers working in partnership have cleared the very invasive Sea-buckthorn from some of the dunes. This clearance work has allowed many plants that grow best on these newly exposed sandy soils to thrive again. Bugloss *Anchusa arvensis,* and Hound's-tongue *Cynoglossum officinale,* in particular, have appeared in large quantities, along with Wild Mignonette *Reseda lutea* and Great Mullein *Verbascum thapsus.* The very large and spectacular Cotton Thistle *Onopordum acanthium* has also benefited from this clearance work. This plant is generally regarded as a garden escape although there is archaeological evidence that it has been in Britain since the Iron Age.

The abundance and range of plant life on the dunes supports an equally wide range of insect life. A good selection of butterflies has been recorded here and several hundred species of moth. Berrow Dunes is also an important site for grasshoppers, crickets, beetles and spiders.

During high summer some of the most obvious butterflies to be seen are the Common

Blue *Polyommatus icarus,* Marbled White *Melanargia galathea,* Meadow Brown *Maniola jurtina,* and Gatekeeper *Pyronia tithonus* together with the very distinctive, and day flying, red-and-black Cinnabar *Tyria jacobaeae* and Six-spot Burnet *Zygaena filipendulae* moths.

Two species of butterfly, the Wall *Lasiommata megera* and Grayling *Hipparchia semele,* are very much creatures of hot, bare-ground habitats, and within Berrow Dunes there are many sunny, sheltered hollows which provide ideal conditions for them to thrive. Despite this, both species have declined considerably in recent years, at Berrow and also across the UK.

Many insects, including butterflies, wasps, bees, ants and beetles, do best in warm, sunny conditions and the mosaic of dune microhabitats found at Brean Dunes make this one of Somerset's most important and exciting places to look for some of our smaller wildlife.

Despite the problems that Sea-buckthorn, Blackthorn and Hawthorn cause by invading the dunes and shading out open ground plant species, the scrubby thickets they form do have merits, particularly for bird life. During the summer the dense, thorny scrub provides safe and secluded feeding and breeding areas for many birds including Linnet *Carduelis cannabina,* Bullfinch *Pyrrhula pyrrhula,* Greenfich *Carduelis chloris,* Long-tailed Tit *Aegithalos caudatus,* Chiffchaff *Phylloscopus collybita,* Willow Warbler *Phylloscopus trochilus,* Whitethroat *Sylvia communis* and Blackcap *Sylvia attricapila.*

◀ **Hare's-foot Clover** *Trifolium arvense*, **Berrow Dunes**, occurs most commonly between Minehead and Brean Down.

Hound's-tongue *Cynoglossum officinale*, **Berrow Dunes**, also found at Dunster Beach. ▶

◀ **Common bird's-foot-trefoil** *Lotus corniculatus*, **Dunster Beach**, a common plant along the coast and inland on many grassy areas.

Male Common Blue *Polyommatus icarus*, **Dunster Beach**, found along the whole coast ▶

Marbled White *Melanargia galathea*, **Berrow Dunes**, found on most grassy places along the coast. ▶

In the winter the orange berries of the Sea-buckthorn are an important food source for Redwing *Turdus iliacus* and Fieldfare *Turdus pilaris* that come to Somerset as winter visitors from northern Europe. Visitors to Berrow Dunes during late afternoon in December and January, just as the light is fading, can see a real wildlife spectacle. Hundreds of Redwings and Fieldfares join large numbers of very noisy Starlings to feast on Sea-buckthorn berries before going to roost for the night in the spiky undergrowth.

At Berrow the sand dunes form a series of ridges parallel to the sea with the newest dunes at the front and the oldest at the back. The long, linear depressions between the dunes are known as 'swales', while the circular and more pond-like damp depressions are known as 'slacks'.

These swales and slacks are often quite damp, as the water table is not far below the surface, particularly during winter and spring. Both temporary and permanent ponds can be found, and in some of the larger wet regions substantial areas of marsh have developed.

At Berrow Dunes, as in many other areas of the UK, the water table has dropped substantially in the last 50 years. This is due to drainage schemes for improving nearby agricultural land, and to the abstraction of groundwater for use in homes. It has led to the complete loss of some dune slack ponds and to others drying out more frequently during the summer. To help compensate for the drop in

water levels some of the ponds have been dredged to lower them and reconnect them with the water table which now lies about half a metre below the surface.

Plants found in these wet areas include Marsh Pennywort *Hydrocotyle vulgaris*, Wild Celery *Apium graveolens*, Parsley Water-dropwort *Oenanthe lachenalii*, Common Fleabane *Pulicaria dysenterica*, Marsh Helleborine *Epipactis palustris*, Early Marsh-orchid *Dactylorhiza incarnata* and Southern Marsh-orchid *Dactylorhiza praetermissa*.

One of the dune slacks here is home to one of the UK's rarest plants, Round-headed Club-rush *Scirpoides holoschoenus,* which is found only at Berrow Dunes and at Braunton Burrows, Devon, in similar habitat.

Despite the precarious nature of pond life among such dry sand dunes, both plants and animals thrive here. Fourteen species of dragonfly have been recorded at Berrow Dunes freshwater wetlands, including the Hairy Dragonfly *Brachytron pratense* and the Ruddy Darter *Sympetrum sanguineum*. A good number of water beetles are also found here including the nationally rare Greater Silver Diving Beetle *Hydrophilus piceus*.

There are several areas of reedbed at Berrow mainly comprising Common Reed *Phragmites australis*. Growing with the reeds are Bulrush *Typha latifolia*, also known as Reed-mace and the considerably rarer Lesser Bulrush *Typha angustifolia*.

Recent recording work has shown these reedbeds to be particularly important habitats for insects including a wide range of moths. Those recorded at Berrow dunes include the Mother Shipton *Callistega mi*, Starwort moth *Cucullia asteris* and Striped Hawkmoth *Hyles lineata livornica*.

These dense reedbeds provide important breeding habitats for the summer migrant Sedge Warbler *Acrocephalus schoenobaenus*, Reed Warbler *Acrocephalus scirpaceus* and Cetti's Warbler *Cettia cetti*. The Bearded Tit *Panarus biarmicus*, one of the UK's rarest breeding birds, also occurs here but only in very small numbers, with only one or two pairs breeding in recent years. Fortunately, the large areas of reedbed found on the Somerset Levels nearby are just right for this reedbed specialist, but total numbers of Bearded Tits in Somerset still amount to only four or five breeding pairs.

Bitterns *Botaurus stellaris* are periodic winter visitors to the Berrow reedbeds, travelling from their summer breeding sites on the Levels, as are Snipe *Gallinago gallinago* and occasionally Woodcock *Scolopax rusticola*.

Similar areas of coastal reedbed occur at Steart and at the mouths of the Rivers Brue and Huntspill, as well as inland at Pawlett Hams. Other smaller areas of reeds occur along stream edges and in ditches and ponds, particularly at Stolford, Lilstock, Doniford, between Blue Anchor and Dunster Beach, at Porlock and

◀ **Hemp-agrimony** *Eupatorium cannabinum*, **dune slacks, Berrow Dunes**, often found along the coast where streams cross the beach.

Southern Marsh-orchid *Dactyorhiza praetermissa*, **dune slacks, Berrow Dunes**. ▶

◀ **Common Fleabane** *Pulicaria dysenterica*, **dune slack, Berrow Dunes**, likes damp grassy places

Sedge Warbler *Acrocephalus schoenobaenus*, **reedbed, Berrow Dunes**, returning to its nest with food for chicks ▶

at what remains of Minehead Marsh.

Although most of these reedbeds are very small they add a great deal to the variety of habitats available for wildlife on the coast. Many are long and narrow, often just the width of the ditch they occupy. Large or small, they all contribute to the diversity and special character of the coast. They also provide wonderful impenetrable places for wildlife to hide away. In addition to nesting Reed and Sedge Warblers, Reed Buntings *Emberiza schoeniclus* occur just about everywhere that reeds are found.

As well as being important places for wildlife these reedbeds add enormously to the attractiveness of the coast. In winter the sun turns them a warm golden colour and they sigh, swish and rattle as the winter winds blow through them. They are a transient habitat that will eventually turn into dry land through the deposition of annual dead reed material. Shrubs and trees will eventually set seed into them

Female Reed Bunting *Emberiza schoeniclus*, edge of Steart reedbed, puffed up for warmth on a very cold winter's day.

and gain a foothold which will speed up the progression to dry land. Where the water supply in a reedbed is generous, periodic flooding to a higher level will kill colonising shrub and tree species.

Traditionally, many reedbeds were regularly cut to provide reeds for thatched cottages and houses. This cutting and removing of the reeds was a major factor in the continued existence of the reed bed and lack of cutting in recent times has led to the loss of much of this type of habitat.

Dunster Beach to Minehead

The sandy upper shore between Dunster Beach and Minehead still holds a wealth of wildlife despite being a very much smaller area of dunes than those found at Burnham and Berrow. The sand and shingle banks in front of the holiday chalets at Dunster Beach have a rich dune flora which is at its most spectacular in June and July when the Viper's-bugloss *Echium vulgare*, Fragrant Evening-primrose, Common Bird's-foot-trefoil and Common Vetch *Vicia sativa* combine to make a vivid display.

The quantity of flora on all dune areas tends to vary depending on the movement of the sand. Sometimes plants disappear under the blown sand, and at other times new species arrive or new combinations of plants spring up.

Despite the variability of the plants that occur from year to year, a summer walk along the coast path between Minehead

and Dunster Beach is always a rewarding experience. As well as Evening-primrose and Viper's Bugloss, Weld *Reseda luteola*, Fennel *Foeniculum vulgare*, Alexanders *Smyrnium olusatrum*, Biting Stonecrop *Sedum acre*, English Stonecrop *Sedum anglicum* and Sea Clover *Trifolium squamosum* are all likely to be found. The Minehead golf course lies adjacent to the sandy coast path between Dunster Beach and Minehead and the dune flora regularly strays onto the course, only occasionally surviving the regular mowing regime. Despite this mowing, the Sand Catchfly *Silene conica* occurs here at its only Somerset site, as does the Slender Thistle *Carduus tenuiflorus* which has a very restricted distribution on Somerset's coast.

These beach areas are, understandably, visited and enjoyed by many thousands of holiday makers during the summer. Inevitably this number of visitors has led to changes in the flora due to trampling pressure, and to the near disappearance as breeding birds of species like Ringed Plovers and Oystercatchers on this stretch of the coast.

Despite all these pressures, it is gratifying to visit the beach directly in front of Minehead Promenade in the middle of July, with hundreds of summer visitors buying ice-creams just a stone's throw away, and still find large amounts of the coast plant specialist Prickly Saltwort *Salsola kali* growing on the sand dunes. In Cornwall, Prickly Saltwort has been lost from most of its sandy beach habitat due to visitor pressure.

Fennel *Foeniculum vulgare*, **Dunster Beach**, probably brought to Britain by the Romans and now very much at home on Somerset's beaches.

White Stonecrop *Sedum album*, **Dunster Beach**, grows on sand, shingle and cliffs.

Viper's-bugloss *Echium vulgare*, **Dunster Beach**, a scarce plant in Somerset, also found at Minehead sands.

Prickly Saltwort *Salsola kali*, **Minehead dunes**.

ROCK AND BOULDER UPPER SHORES

Between Blue Anchor and Hinkley Point much of the upper beach is composed of fairly flat, but convoluted and broken rock platforms. These are known as 'wave-cut platforms', having been eroded by the sea. They are made of Jurassic Blue Lias stone.

Lying on top of these platforms are varying amounts of shingle that are continuously moved around by the sea. There are also quantities of rock here and very large boulders that have recently fallen from the cliffs behind.

The sea washes right across these rocky beaches, reaching the low cliffs on most tides. This makes it a dangerous place to walk unless you know exactly what the tide is doing. This danger is magnified by the very slow rate of progress that you can make across such uneven terrain.

Given that the sea travels right across the beach and touches the lower cliff so regularly it is no surprise that no land plants make their home

on this part of the beach. The swift rate of erosion from the lower and middle parts of the cliff also precludes much colonisation by plants.

Rock Pipit *Anthus petrosus*, Wren *Troglodytes troglodytes* and Pied Wagtail *Motacilla alba* are the birds most often seen scuttling around the upper parts of these rugged beaches, all intent on finding invertebrate food hidden in cracks and crevices.

Lower down the beach groups of Jackdaws *Corvus monedula* and Carrion Crows *Corvus corone corone* spend many hours, particularly during the winter when food is short, hunting for anything edible in the large amounts of tideline debris that gets caught on the rocks. They also search in the shallower rock pools for small marine creatures, dead or alive. Rooks *Corvus frugilegus* seem to make it down onto the beach much less often than other members of the crow family, but Ravens *Corvus corax* are resident along this

stretch of the coast and very much in evidence most days. The harsh and very loud 'cronk' call of the Raven echoes wonderfully off the cliffs here, matching very well the rather unyielding, rocky nature of this part of Somerset's coast.

The natural, rocky defences along this stretch of beach keep visitor numbers fairly low, and as a result are partly responsible for making this beach so attractive to Ravens. The other attraction for Ravens here is the safe nesting ledges on cliffs high up at the back of the beach.

The lack of disturbance on these beaches also allows the Peregrine *Falco peregrinus* to spend considerable time hunting along these shores. They can often be seen here, perching on large boulders, while they keep an intent watch over the beach. There are good chances for them to catch unwary birds here as they feed along the shore, particularly in winter time.

SHINGLE BANKS

The sound of waves lapping against shingle banks can be very evocative. On a calm day, the sea moving gently between the pebbles can be soporific, while at other times it can scare when the power of the waves shifts a great section of the pebble beach into a new shape in front of your eyes or sucks

the very pebbles you are standing on out from under your feet.

Areas of shingle are found heaped up against the cliffs or on the mid and lower parts of many Somerset beaches, but substantial, freestanding shingle ridges occur only at Steart, Stolford, Porlock, Porlock

Weir, between Blue Anchor Bay and Dunster Beach and at Lilstock.

The nature of a shingle bank is to shift and move. Sometimes the shingle moves only slightly with each tide. At other times it moves dramatically following stormy weather when heavy seas

◄ **Juvenile Pied Wagtail** *Motacilla alba*, **Stolford beach**. Note the slightly yellow face that these young birds often have.

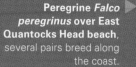
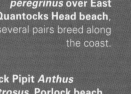

Peregrine *Falco peregrinus* **over East Quantocks Head beach,** ► several pairs breed along the coast.

◄ **Rock Pipit** *Anthus petrosus*, **Porlock beach,** hunting for invertebrate food along the tideline.

Raven *Corvus corvax*, ► **Porlock** found along all the beaches with cliffs behind them.

batter the coast or when a 'spring tide' occurs.

A spring tide occurs when the difference between high and low tide is greatest. Spring tides occur when the moon is either new or full and the sun, the moon, and the Earth are aligned. When this is the case, their collective gravitational pull on the Earth's seas is strengthened. A spring tide not only gives rise to a very high tide coming up the beach; it also means the tide drops extra low at low tide, making this a good time to explore rockpools that are not exposed very often.

Some of these shingle ridges have been modified, or partly modified, to create more robust sea defences to protect low-lying land behind them from flooding by the sea. This is achieved by pushing the shingle into a higher ridge with heavy machinery on a regular basis. This used to be carried out at Porlock and is still done between Stolford and Wall Common. Some ridges have had large, non-local stone boulders added to their lower seaward slopes to stop high tides breaking through the banks. This has been done east of Hinkley Point. Others have been partly modified by putting the larger stones from the shingle into wire-mesh boxes called 'gabions', and then stacking them at the back of the shingle bank to try to ensure that the bank remains in position. This has been done at Lilstock.

In many ways the wildlife of Somerset's shingle beaches has been considerably less affected by human activities than the sand beaches. The shingle banks are hard work to walk on

and their rather unforgiving nature means they have been spared much of the impact of leisure activities and commercial holiday developments that the sand beaches experience.

Porlock shingle bank

The shingle bank that stretches between Porlock Weir and Hurlstone Point is the longest in Somerset at just on 5 km. Until 1996 the shingle here formed a continuous ridge between Porlock Weir and Hurlstone Point. Up to this date the ridge had been subject to periodic repairs by bulldozing the shingle back into position whenever stormy seas threatened to break through it. The aim of the repair work was to protect the grazing land behind the ridge from being flooded with sea water.

During a severe storm in October 1996 a very substantial breach was made in the shingle by heavy seas which in turn led to considerable flooding of the grazing marsh. Following consultation with the National Trust who own the eastern end of the ridge, and with the Exmoor National Park Authority, English Nature and local landowners, it was decided to follow a policy of 'managed retreat'. The sea, the shingle ridge and the land behind the ridge will be allowed to work out their own equilibrium. Allowing this area to follow its natural course could well result in a reversion to the situation of around 200 years ago. Maps of that period show a breached ridge and lagoon instead of a marsh.

The breach through the shingle ridge at Porlock is a

fascinating place to visit. It takes on a different shape almost every day as the tide moves through it, creating ever-changing, small-scale, estuary-type landscapes. In particular, the shingle headlands and mini islands that come and go within the breach are often sought out as safe places to rest by waders on spring and autumn migrations.

The Porlock shingle seems to hold a great attraction for Wheatears *Oenanthe oenanthe* and this is a regular place to find them on their spring and autumn migration. Rock Pipits, which are resident and breed here, are also fairly easy to see as they forage for insects among the debris of the upper tidelines.

Although not common, Rock Pipits are found along most of the shingle and rocky beaches on Somerset's coast. They usually nest in holes or crevices in rocks and shingle at the back of the beach, and often where the spray from higher tides is bound to reach them.

Meadow Pipits *Anthus pratensis* are also regular visitors to the shingle banks, where they hunt for small insects among the beach debris. This is particularly the case when salt marsh or grassland, which Meadow Pipits favour, is found immediately behind the shingle beaches.

Rock Pipits and Meadow Pipits are very similar, but Rock Pipits are larger, 15.5–17 cm in length, as opposed to Meadow Pipits which are 14–15.5 cm in length. Rock Pipits have a duller, more sombre, grey-brown plumage and dark-coloured legs as opposed to pink, flesh-coloured ones. They also have a

◄ **Sea Campion** *Silene uniflora*, **Porlock shingle bank**, also found on cliffs at Brean Down.

Sea Beet *Beta vulgaris* **subspecies** *maritima*, **Stolford**, the plant that Beetroot was developed from. ►

Scarlet Pimpernel *Anagallis arvensis*, **Porlock Weir**, common along much of the coast. ►

Thrift *Armeria maritima*, **Porlock shingle ridge**, also found on the drier parts of saltmarsh. ►

considerably heavier bill than the Meadow Pipit.

Shingle can appear to be an almost impossible place for plants to grow but many do gain a foothold, usually towards the back of the highest part of the ridge, and then more abundantly on the landward slope.

The plant life here has to be tough and well-adapted to living on the shingle. Most plants survive by having roots that reach deep down to the fresh water that seeps through the shingle. This water comes from several streams that run off the hill slopes behind Porlock itself. It filters through the marshy ground behind the shingle before passing through it and out towards the sea.

Even the tiny, low-growing Scarlet Pimpernel *Anagallis arvensis*, which grows quite abundantly across the shingle, has roots that reach down for at least 50 cm to reach fresh water.

Sea Beet *Beta vulgaris* subspecies *maritima* is one of the most common, but least showy, of the shingle specialist plants. It is a perennial that forms dense, dark green, shiny-leaved, ground-hugging mounds, that by the end of the summer may be 1.5 metres in diameter. Many plants cannot tolerate salt spray on their leaves. Sea Beet, however, has very waxy leaves which are excellent at shedding salt spray and it is often the plant that grows lowest down the beach, very close to where the higher tides reach.

Sea Beet is also a fascinating plant because of the role that it has played in the development of some of our common foodstuffs. Over thousands of years, and through very careful

selective breeding of this rather humble plant, we have produced Beet Spinach, Mangolds and Beetroot.

Another plant found here is Thrift, or Sea Pink, *Armeria maritima*. It occurs sparingly along the entire Somerset coast, but undoubtedly is at its most abundant around the middle point of the Porlock shingle bank. This may well be due to a lack of easy access here, as it is prone to being picked in more easily reached places. Sea Campion *Silene uniflora* is another plant that can be found along the whole coast but again grows abundantly on the Porlock shingle ridge.

Making the effort to visit the remoter parts of this amazing landscape is worthwhile at any time of year, but a visit in high summer can be particularly special.

On a bright sunny day it can have a strange, otherworldly feel about it; huge areas of shingle with few significant distinguishing features can make it a disorientating place to visit. It is uncomfortable to walk on and initially appears an unpromising place to find much wildlife.

This is deceptive. At your feet, much of the shingle will have lichen growing on it. The clean and damp, south-westerly sea breezes that blow across this coast create ideal conditions for many species of lichens to thrive. Huge areas of shingle can be covered with the Sunburst Lichen *Xanthoria parietina* which forms a crust on the stones and is a bright, almost psychedelic, orange. Many other species of lichen can be found here with careful searching,

On still days the sheltered, landward, south-facing slope of the shingle ridge can be very hot. Large patches of Common Bird's-foot-trefoil, Sea Campion and Thrift hug the shingle tightly and provide nectar for many visiting insects. Butterflies such as Red Admiral *Vanessa atalanta*, Small Tortoiseshell *Aglais urticae*, Painted Lady *Vanessa cardui* and Common Blue seem to find this a favourite summer haunt year after year. You are certain to hear Skylarks *Alauda arvensis* high overhead and Barn Swallows *Hirundo rustica* often fly low along the ridge feeding on the many small insects attracted to the flowering plants.

The shingle beach at Porlock Weir

At the western end of the Porlock shingle bank lies Porlock Weir. Many of the beachside cottages here have gardens that are literally part of the beach. This has given rise to an amazing shingle vegetation. You will find a mixture of plants native to Somerset's coast as well as garden plants from southern Europe that are at home in dry, stony environments. Growing straight out of the shingle, and looking very much at home are the garden plants Snapdragon *Antirrhinum majus*, Purple Toadflax *Linarea purpurea*, Red Valerian *Centranthus ruber* and Wallflower *Cheiranthus cheiri* which all come from southern Europe or the coasts of the Mediterranean.

One of the native, but exotic-looking, beach plants that grows here is Tree-mallow *Lavatera arborea*. This tall, 200 cm, woody plant grows

Wallflowers *Cheiranthus cheiri*, **Porlock Weir**, a garden escape but recorded in the wild since the 1500s.

Red Valerian *Centranthus ruber*, **Porlock Weir**, another garden escape very happy on the beach.

Sunburst Lichen *Xanthoria parietina*, **Porlock Weir, with Sea Milkwort** *Glaux maritima*, this lichen occurs on most stony and rocky beaches.

Tree-mallow *Lavatera arborea*, **Porlock Weir**, a native plant on south western coasts.

Yellow Horned-poppy *Glaucium flavum,* **Dunster Beach**, a plant only ever found on the coast.

Ringed Plover *Chardrius hiaticula,* **Steart,** this is the habitat they like to nest in, if undisturbed. ▶

◀ **Musk Stork's-bill** *Erodium moschatum,* **Wall Common**, a very low growing plant and often overlooked.

◀ **Sea Mayweed** *Tripleurospermum maritimum,* **Dunster Beach**, fairly common along the coast on sand and shingle.

Oystercatchers ▶ *Haematopus ostralegus* **and sleeping Turnstone** *Arenaria interpres,* **Stolford**. Oystercatches are along the coast all year, a small number breed others are winter visitors.

naturally on the south-west coasts of the UK and was taken into cultivation many years ago. It is intolerant of frost and hardly ever grows more than 100 metres from the sea. It has roots that may stretch down for 150 cm to reach fresh water, which make it well suited to Porlock's stony habitat.

Other shingle ridges

Somerset's other, and smaller, shingle ridges and beaches are all well worth visiting to hunt for their fascinating wildlife. They share many of the plants that are found at Porlock. Those to look out for include Yellow Horned-poppy *Glaucium flavum* which grows no further east or north on Somerset's coast than Steart and was last recorded at Burnham in 1924; Common Restharrow *Ononis repens*, Shinning Crane's-bill *Geranium lucidum*, Musk Stork's-bill *Erodium moschatum*, Sea Mayweed *Tripleurospermum maritimum*, Navelwort *Umbelicus rupestris* and Sea Plantain *Plantago maritima*.

Bittersweet *Solanum dulcamara* is a well-known woodland-edge plant that often climbs up to between two and three metres on woodland shrubs. On shingle beaches, however, a low-growing form *Solanum dulcamara* var. *marinum* is found which is happy growing on its own far from its usual shady habitat. Its bright red berries are very noticeable in late summer.

There is another member of the Solanaceae or Potato family that occurs periodically along Somerset's coast on shingle, sand and grassy clifftops. This is the Duke of Argyll's Tea-plant *Lycium barbarum*. It is a native

of China and gets its name from being, mistakenly, identified in the 18th century as a bush whose leaves could be used for making tea. It has often been used for hedging gardens in coastal areas. Many birds are keen to eat its berries and then carry its seed to wilder places.

Several species of thistle may appear on these shingle banks. This is not surprising as thistles are very adept at invading bare ground in gardens and on agricultural land. The very common Spear Thistle *Cirsium vulgare* can be found in many shingle areas but the Slender Thistle has a much more limited distribution. It is found at Stolford and on the shingle and sand banks between Dunster Beach and Minehead.

While shingle is not the most welcoming of habitats for humans, over several thousand years large numbers of plants and a number of birds have evolved ways of using this rather tough environment. Rock Pipits are very adept at hiding their nests in crevices, while migratory birds like the Wheatear, drop in briefly to feed on the shingle banks in spring and autumn, finding it quiet enough to feed peacefully most of the time.

However, two species of bird that have made these stony beaches their summer home are not coping well with modern life. Oystercatchers and Ringed Plovers have both evolved eggs that are beautifully camouflaged to match the stones on the very exposed shingle areas that they nest on, as well as habits that help avoid detection of their nests on the shingle by predators.

Both species still nest on these beaches but in tiny

numbers compared to 100 years ago. Their reduction as breeding birds on this coast matches exactly the expansion of coastal holiday developments and the large increase in summer holiday visitors. Although these shingle banks are not so much visited as the sand beaches there is still enough accidental disturbance by beach visitors to cause high losses to eggs and chicks.

Oystercatchers and Ringed Plovers are very much part of the wild heritage of Somerset's coast. Maintaining them now and into the future as breeding birds on several of these beaches would be a tremendous achievement. Aside from Steart Point, part of Bridgwater Bay National Nature Reserve, providing some sanctuary for one or two pairs of Oystercatchers and Ringed Plovers to periodically nest, successful breeding along the rest of the coast is highly debatable.

At the current time there are no specific coastal landscape conservation plans to try and ensure that Oystercatcher and Ringed Plover have successful breeding seasons on these shingle beaches, although both species are on the Priority Species List in the Somerset Biodiversty Action Plan. Being able to provide the space and right conditions for these two species, that hover on the brink of extinction as breeding birds on this coast, to thrive, would be a tremendous achievement and symbolic of the enthusiasm and commitment of the many individuals and organisations concerned with Somerset's wildlife and the future well-being of this wonderful coastline.

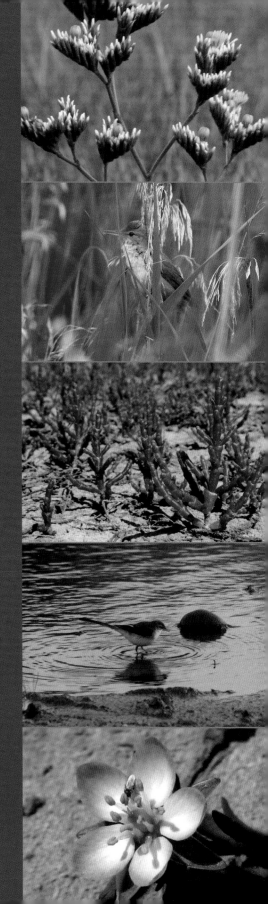

5

Behind the Beach

Sea-purslane *Atriplex portulacoides* and purple Sea Aster *Aster tripolium*, Porlock Marsh.

Common Sea-lavender *Limonium vulgare*, Wall Common.

Reed Warbler *Acrocephalus scirpaceus*, reedbed, Stolford.

Common Glasswort *Salicornia europaea*, Wall Common.

Grey Wagtail *Motacilla cinerea*, saltmarsh pool, Stolford.

Greater Sea-spurrey *Spergularia media*, Porlock Marsh.

SALTMARSHES AND HOW THEY WORK

Saltmarshes are those very flat, very low vegetation, areas that lie behind several Somerset beaches. They often have intricate sinuous water channels that are created by the seawater as it drains back towards the sea following flooding.

The water channels can be very narrow, deep and partly hidden by the vegetation. Deep areas of mud can look like firm ground. Saltmarsh has a reputation for being unsafe for humans. This is of course one of its great strengths for wildlife, particularly for birds. Few species attempt to breed here, but as an undisturbed and safe place to feed, saltmarshes play a very important role for birds seeking invertebrate and plant food, particularly during the winter months.

Saltmarshes become established on low-lying areas of sand and mud, often on land behind a shingle or sand dune barrier that prevents the sea from reaching them, or are only irregularly inundated by the sea. They may only be washed by the sea at spring tides which occur twice each month or during storm conditions. This is a harsh environment which can only be colonised by a limited range of land plants that have a high tolerance of salty conditions.

If conditions are good, with the right slope on the beach, saltmarsh can also develop on the higher parts of the beach. This is the case between Wall Common and Steart, but there is also saltmarsh behind the shingle and sandbank here too.

The saltmarshes found along the Stolford, Wall Common and Steart coast comprise the largest area of saltmarsh remaining in Somerset. Smaller areas are found at Porlock Weir at the upper end of the small harbour and around the mouths of the rivers Huntspill, Parrett, Brue and Axe, just north of Brean. The large area of marshland behind the shingle bank at Porlock was, until 1996, mainly a freshwater grazing marsh. Following the breach by the sea in the shingle bank that year, this land is now regularly flooded with sea water and large areas are changing into saltmarsh.

The periodic inundation by salt water of these marshes severely limits the number of plants here. Only those that can tolerate high levels of salt survive. Periodic invasion by the salt water very much slows down or completely precludes the sort of succession that can take place in freshwater marshes. In fresh water, shrubs and trees will eventually gain a foothold and the annual fall of leaf litter will gradually turn the marsh into dry land. In a saltmarsh the sea washing across the marsh, even just a couple of times each month, has a devastating effect on any plant life that is not highly adapted to cope with it.

The Somerset coast has had a number of sea walls or barriers constructed along its length during the last 200 years. Some protect towns like Burnham, but most were built to stop the sea flooding across the low-lying farmed land behind the beach. Once these walls are in place the saltmarsh vegetation is replaced by naturally-colonising, freshwater meadow species, many of which are more palatable to livestock than the salt-hardy plants. This allows the meadows to be grazed more regularly with livestock. Some of this land has then had considerable drainage and ditching work carried out on it and is now dry enough to be used for growing crops.

The total amount of saltmarsh that has been lost following the creation of sea defences is unknown but it is likely that what we have left is a tiny proportion of what once existed. The most recent, documented, loss of this habitat was at Minehead in 1962 when the Butlin's holiday camp was built on roughly 100 hectares of saltmarsh that lay just behind the beach.

Saltmarshes are the naturally-occurring buffer zones between the beach and the 'real' dry land. They are in-between places, not pleasant to walk on, or high and dry enough to build on. They have always been seen as waste land; to be targeted for drainage schemes and used for 'proper' agriculture, or as places to house sewage works or rubbish dumps. But without saltmarsh buffer zones it is going to be increasingly hard to cope with the sea-level rise that we are experiencing already. Along parts of Somerset's coast and many other of the UK's low-lying coastal areas, it is likely that the most cost-effective way of coping with higher seas and storm surges will be to recreate these natural places that are so good at soaking up the extra high tides.

◀ **Saltmarsh, Stolford**, a natural flood defence system.

River Axe saltmarsh, Weston-Super-Mare in the background. ▶

Due to rising sea levels the saltmarsh at Wall Common is rapidly eroding. ▶

Porlock Marsh, where ▶ the sea has only been allowed to flood in since the mid 1990s.

PLANTS IN THE SALTMARSH

There are often very distinct lower and upper vegetation zones in saltmarsh. Upper saltmarsh areas can be dominated by a mixture of the grass Red Fescue *Festuca rubra* ssp. *litoralis* and Common Saltmarsh-grass *Puccinellia maritima*, both of which can tolerate a fair splashing of saltwater. The lower parts of the marsh may be covered with Common Cord-grass *Spartina anglica*, also known as Spartina Grass which can cope with several hours of inundation by the sea each week.

Plants that can tolerate high levels of salt and periodic immersion by the sea are called halophytes. Common Cord-grass is most certainly a halophyte, but perhaps some of the best-known and easily-identifiable halophytes are the Glassworts. They are strange plants that looks like succulents and appear to have no leaves or flowers. They grow out of the bare mud very low down the shore and taste deliciously salty.

Common Glasswort *Salicornia europaea* is the species most likely to be found growing in the Bridgwater Bay saltmarshes. Purple Glasswort *Salicornia ramosissima*, Long-spiked Glasswort *Salicornia dolichostachya* and One-flowered Glasswort *Salicornia pusilla* are also known to occur along this coast but are rather hard to tell apart.

Glassworts do have leaves but they are very small and clasp the stem like scales. They also have flowers, but

again these are very tiny, usually occurring in clusters of three and lying close to each leaf scale.

Berrow

Although rather swamped by the encroaching Sea-buckthorn *Hippophae rhamnoides*, there is an area of saltmarsh at Berrow. It lies immediately behind the dunes and roughly opposite Berrow church. Around 100 years ago there was enough of a gap in the dunes here to allow the sea to regularly flood through and create the saltmarsh.

Now, however, the direct influence of the sea on this area is very small, as new dunes have formed and closed the gap. Despite this the marsh still has a strong saltmarsh flora including Common Cord-grass, Saltmarsh Rush *Juncus gerardi*, Sea Club-rush *Bolboschoenus maritimus*, Common Saltmarsh-grass, Sea Milkwort *Glaux maritima*, Sea Arrowgrass *Triglochin maritima*, Common Sea-lavender *Limonium vulgare* and Sea Aster *Aster tripolium*.

Stolford to Steart

This is one of the best places to become familiar with saltmarsh wildlife. Walking the coast path here will allow you to see a great variety of saltmarsh plants without straying into deep mud, and many are distinctive and easy to identify. One particularly plant-rich area along this path is Wall Common which lies about midway between Stolford and Steart Point. Sea Wormwood

Seriphidium maritimum, Common Sea-lavender, Common Scurvy-grass *Cochlearia officinalis* and Spear-leaved Orache *Atriplex prostrata* can all be found growing abundantly here.

Wall Common is also another very good example of changing habitats along the coast. It shows how dynamic the coast landscape can be and how good some plant species are at exploiting new habitats. New deposits of sand are starting to accumulate here on top of traditional saltmarsh areas. The sand is being blown from lower down the beach and is likely to eventually dry out this particular piece of saltmarsh if it carries on at the current rate. At the moment it gives rise to plants such as Sea Spurge *Euphorbia paralias* and Sea Sandwort *Honkenya peploides*, both new sand dune pioneers, growing on tiny dune areas in amongst the Glasswort.

The other great change to the saltmarsh vegetation here concerns Cord-grass, which occurs in quite large areas on the seaward side of the shingle bank. Cord-grass was planted extensively in the Bridgwater Bay area in the early 1930s to help stabilise areas of mudflats.

Thousands of plants were planted by hand on the shallow, muddy beaches with the intention that the young plants would catch sediment that was carried in by the tides. As the sediment built up, new higher land would be created and the shore would in effect creep forward. This would

Common Glasswort *Salicornia europaea,* **Wall Common**, by late summer it changes from green to this redish pink colour.

Sea Milkwort *Glaux maritima,* **Porlock Marsh**, very low growing and easy to overlook.

Common Sea-lavender *Limonium vulgare,* **Wall Common**, most abundant on the drier saltmarsh.

Sea Wormwood *Seriphidium maritimum,* **Wall Common**, a striking silvery white plant of the drier saltmarsh.

Common Cord-grass *Spartina anglica*, **Wall Common**, highly resistant to salt water and often planted as part of flood defence schemes.

Sea Aster *Aster tripolium*, **Porlock Marsh**, closely related to many of our garden Asters

Sea Plantain *Plantago maritima*, **Porlock Weir**, grows at the edge of the saltmarsh and other bare ground close to the sea.

Sea Club-rush *Bolboschoenus maritimus*, **Porlock Weir**, a robust patch forming plant of brakish water.

then, in turn, lead to greater protection from flooding at places such as Wall Common and Steart for the grazing marshes and farms behind the beach.

Cord-grass occurs naturally along much of the southern coastline of the UK but it has been used extensively in planting schemes designed to reduce erosion of the foreshore at many coastal sites. It is an extremely salt-hardy plant and can tolerate complete submergence under the sea for long periods.

This 'flood defense' saltmarsh scheme that the Cord-grass created worked successfully for a considerable time. The very robust root system of the Cord-grass was effective at binding the newly deposited silt together and hence encouraging other saltmarsh plants to colonise.

However, in the last 15 years the rise in sea level that has occurred, albeit only a few extra millimetres a year, has led to a considerable amount of this middle beach saltmarsh being washed away. At Wall Common the saltmarsh has been eroded back towards the shingle bank by around 300 metres. This loss of the saltmarsh, whose vegetation once bound the silts and sands together over such a large area, is the most likely cause of the new sand now appearing on the saltmarsh behind the shingle bank.

Another example of how saltmarsh vegetation can develop occurs along the upper beach at Steart. Here Common Reed *Phragmites australis* has colonised a 2-km long section of the upper saltmarsh creating a dense wall of reeds bordering the coast path that leads from Wall Common towards Steart. Common Reed does not have a great tolerance for salt water and with the tide reaching ever higher up the beach, this reed bed may unfortunately have a fairly limited lifespan.

Porlock Weir

Porlock Weir is another site with exceptionally good access to the saltmarsh along the coast path that heads west from the small harbour.

A large part of the lower areas of saltmarsh here are dominated by Sea-purslane *Atriplex portulacoides*. This forms extensive, grey-leaved and low-growing mats of vegetation that at first sight appear rather featureless. Close up, the leaves have a silvery-white sheen which is caused by a coating of fine white scales on both sides of the leaves. Sea-purslane's flowers are very tiny, a greenish yellow, and found on small spikes at the tip of the plant between July and October.

Because so few plants can cope with this salt environment, those that do grow here often have relatively little competition which often leads to one plant, such as Sea-purslane in this case, covering such large areas.

On slightly higher ground in the marsh, above the Sea-purslane dominated areas, Sea Arrowgrass occurs in large patches. This plant is not a grass but is so named because of its narrow grass-like leaves. In the same raised, and in consequence slightly less salty, areas are dense thickets of Sea Club-rush. A specialist of brackish water, it is hardly ever found growing in fresh water.

As the marsh starts to merge into the shingle bank on its seaward side, and gets a little drier, plants of the upper saltmarsh start to appear including Sea Milkwort, Greater Sea-spurrey *Spergularia media* and Sea Plantain.

Behind the Porlock shingle bank

This is a wonderfully large and fairly hazardous area of saltmarsh. Up until 1996 it was a freshwater grazing marsh with small areas of saltmarsh occurring immediately behind the shingle bank. During a very severe storm in that year the sea broke through the shingle bank, and since that time the sea continues to flood across the marsh on most high tides.

Because this is a relatively new invasion of the area by the sea, the water that comes in on the high tides can move about in a rather erratic way. Regular channels, where the water flows onto the marsh and then flows off again, are not yet fully established. This can give rise to situations where,what was a dry path one day can be completely submerged the next, so great care needs to be taken when visiting the area.

The salt water has caused the death of hedges and trees that once grew here, and the once substantial reedbed too has all but disappeared. Fortunately Somerset is very well endowed with hedges and reedbeds, and to gain such a substantial area of saltmarsh is a huge benefit for coastal wildlife.

On the inland, and much grassier side of the marsh, Sea

Aster covers large areas and makes a terrific display in August and September. It always seems a surprise to see this plant that has so many well-known garden relatives, growing so happily in such a rough place. As at Porlock Weir, Sea Purslane now covers considerable areas of the marsh but there is enough open ground for the bare area specialists Common Glasswort, Annual Seablite *Suaeda maritima*, and Spear-leaved Orache to thrive. On slightly higher and drier parts of the marsh Red Fescue and Sea Milkwort form very extensive 'lawns' that are heavily grazed by rabbits which burrow in some of the higher and drier hedge banks which surround the marsh. Sea Plantain and Sea Arrowgrass also grow in these higher areas.

One of the botanical delights of Porlock Marsh is the area where the saltmarsh meets the rear slope of the shingle ridge. Along a strip around ten metres wide, plants from the two habitats intermingle giving rise to a wonderfully diverse flora. The shingle plants Sea Campion *Silene uniflora*, Thrift *Armeria maritima*, Common Bird's-foot-trefoil *Lotus corniculatus* and Yellow Horned-poppy *Glaucium flavum* creep down the slope to grow among the Sea-purslane and Sea Milkwort of the marsh. In this same area where the shingle ridge is most stable the bright orange, encrusting *Xanthoria* lichen covers large areas of pebbles but there are also more unusual lichens here including *Rinodina aspersa* which is nationally rare and three other species which are nationally scarce *Buellia subdisciformis*, *Caloplaca arnoldii* and *Lecanora subcarnea*.

ANIMALS ON THE SALTMARSH

Birds

The incursion of the sea into Porlock Marsh has created considerably more bare, muddy ground caused by the dieback of several grass species with no tolerance for salt. This new muddy ground is ideal wader-feeding terrain and Redshank *Tringa totanus*, Curlew *Numenius arquata* and Oystercatchers *Haematopus ostralegus* are now found here throughout the year. There are also some higher and drier spots within the marsh on which all three of these species could nest in the future. The Common Snipe *Gallinago gallinago* is also a regular visitor but is often very hard to spot as there are so many dips and hollows in the marsh for the Snipe to hide in.

The marsh's mosaic of muddy pools is very much the sort of habitat that Greenshank *Tringa nebularia* like to drop in on during their spring and autumn migrations. Their visits can be very brief, though, and they are easy to miss. Dunlin *Calidris alpina* also make this a regular migration stopping-point.

This complex network of small pools, ditches and drainage channels is also very attractive to ducks, and Shoveler *Anas clypeata*, Wigeon *Anas penelope* and Teal *Anas crecca* all come here during the winter. Shelduck *Tadorna tadorna* are present throughout the year and have been known to breed here.

Not surprisingly, this is exactly the sort of habitat that Herons *Ardea cinerea* and Little Egrets *Egretta garzetta* thrive on and both species are here throughout the year. The Herons seen here will have come from heronries, where they breed, on the nearby wooded slopes of Exmoor.

The landscape setting of Porlock's saltmarsh is unique. Nearly all saltmarshes in England lie along very flat coastal areas, with some of the biggest concentrations being along the Essex, Suffolk and Norfolk coast. To have the high, and very dramatic, Exmoor landscape bordering the marsh gives this part of Somerset's coast a very special feeling.

The other contribution that Exmoor makes is the large amount of fresh water that runs down its slopes and into the marsh. Horner Water runs into the eastern end of the marsh and another significant stream comes down from Hawke Combe and into the marsh through Porlock itself. The presence of these streams means that the salt water washing onto the saltmarsh will always be moderated by fresh water. This is a

Grey Heron *Ardea cinerea*, **Porlock Marsh**, a bird so at home in this habitat.

Dunlin *Calidris alpina*, **Porlock saltmarsh, May**, a passage migrant in summer plumage, on its way to northern Europe.

Little Grebe *Tachybaptus ruficollis*, **brakish lagoon, Stolford**, breeds here, quite often seen out on the sea at high tide.

◄ **Meadow Pipit *Anthus pratensis*, Wall Common**, breeds on the drier edge of the saltmarsh. Much paler than the Rock Pipits *Anthus petrosus* that may also be found here.

◄ **Skylark *Alauda arvensis*, Wall Common**, breeds on the drier parts of the saltmarsh and close by fields. The slight crest is a good diagnostic feature.

◄ **Starlings *Sternus vulgaris*, Stolford**, a common saltmarsh visitor often in large numbers.

Snow Bunting *Plectrophenax nivalis*, Stolford, winter, a bird ►
that breeds in high mountain habitats in Scandinavia and Greenland and small numbers in Scotland. They spend a lot of time feeding on seeds of Red Fescue grass.

particularly significant factor for plants as it means that much of the freshwater plant life of the marsh will continue here. Over time this will give rise to a more diverse flora than if it was merely a salt or freshwater marsh.

Many of Somerset's saltmarshes are dominated by large areas of grass such as Red Fescue and Common Saltmarsh-grass mixed in with Glasswort. These rather monotonous-looking places do not appear to offer an abundance of food but they do have a great attraction for a number of birds.

In the autumn and winter months Meadow Pipits *Anthus pratensis* can be found feeding on the saltmarsh in large, loose flocks of between 50 and 80 birds. Although some will be local birds, many will have come from the north of England and from Scotland, as well as a few from Europe. It is thought that most Meadow Pipits that breed in mainland Europe travel down to Spain and Portugal during the winter months.

Like many of the other small birds that come to feed on the saltmarshes during the winter Meadow Pipits will be feeding on invertebrates like woodlice, very small spiders and beetles, and the smaller snails and worms. They also spend a lot of time jumping up to pick insects out of the air. The seeds of grasses and Glasswort make up a smaller part of their diet. The fact that the sea is so near ensures that most of the time saltmarsh areas have fairly mild climates. This accounts for insect food being available here when

inland grass areas may be frozen solid.

Meadow Pipits are still on the saltmarsh during summer but in much smaller numbers. They nest on the ground in rough grass and bramble on higher parts of the marsh, and on the grassy earth banks that lie around the boundaries of many of these marshes. They also nest in corners of the grass fields that lie inland of the marsh.

The winter Meadow Pipit flocks are often joined by Skylarks *Alauda arvensis* and Pied Wagtails *Motacilla alba*, all of them racing around, pecking at food items that seem too small to be of great value. They too are mainly feeding on a combination of tiny insects, grass seeds and Glasswort seeds. In the depths of winter they need to feed like this all day long. Very cold weather combined with short daylight hours make this task a race against time to survive each day. The value of saltmarsh to these wintering birds is very high. The slightly higher coastal temperatures combined with the surprisingly abundant food here make them a critical element in the survival strategy for a very considerable number of birds.

Many of the Skylarks seen here during winter will be from other parts of Somerset but many also travel down from north-east Europe to escape the cold. Skylarks are seen on and over many saltmarsh areas throughout the year, with some of them nesting in the higher and drier parts of the marsh. Skylark nests often have no concealment and consist only of a grass-lined hollow on the

bare ground. They depend upon the camouflage of their eggs and of their plumage to keep them safe.

The Somerset Levels are famous for very large flocks, sometimes numbering millions, of wintering Starlings *Sturnus vulgaris*, that roost in the reedbeds at night. Starlings also come to the saltmarshes in large numbers to feed and roost in saltmarsh reed beds. The Starlings on the saltmarshes may only occur in a few thousands but they are still a very impressive sight as they spread out to feed across the marsh like a dark invading army. Many of these Starlings roost in reed beds close to the saltmarshes in groups of a few hundred but they also roost at night in large trees, in hedgerows behind the marsh and sometimes on the roofs of nearby farm buildings.

As with all habitats you can never be sure of what you may find on the saltmarshes. Being so flat they can become very windy. During winter, strong winds and low temperatures can combine to make them an inhospitable place, and with little cover all bird life may suddenly appear to have been swept away.

On still and sunny winter days it can be very different. If the tide is high up the beach many wading birds and duck will come onto the saltmarsh to rest during high tide before returning to feed as the tide retreats. Redshank, Turnstone, Dunlin, Curlew, Oystercatcher, Ringed Plover, Shelduck and Teal all make good use of the Stolford to Steart saltmarshes as a high-tide roost.

Female Kestrel *Falco tinnunculus*, **Porlock Marsh, winter**, prey will include small birds and mammals

Winter flock of Pied Wagtails *Motacilla alba*, Stolford.

Brown Hare *Lepus capensis*, **Wall Common**, a surprisingly frequent visitor to the drier parts of reedbeds behind the beach.

Roe Deer *Capreolus capreolus*, quite often seen on the grazing marshes behind the beach.

The Stolford-to-Steart saltmarshes are also a favourite, regular wintering spot for Snow Buntings *Plectrophenax nivalis*. Snow Buntings have been observed on the Somerset coast since record-keeping started in the early 1800s, and they were probably here long before that. They have been recorded from Brean to Porlock, and the high ground on Exmoor is also another regular place for them.

Snow Buntings are about the size of sparrows. They breed in Iceland, in Greenland and on mainland Europe in the Arctic Circle. As these areas freeze solid and the long dark winter begins they move south. In the UK most Snow Buntings winter on the east coast with just a few travelling to the Somerset coast, currently between ten and 15 birds each winter. Watching them spend hours on the saltmarsh feeding on tiny grass seeds looks like hard work to us but is probably heaven in comparison to an Arctic winter.

In summer and winter the Kestrel *Falco tinnunculus* is the most frequently-seen predatory bird over the marshes. The wind off the sea creates upward currents ideal for the hovering flight that Kestrels are so adept at and this is a favourite place for them to hunt. Sparse saltmarsh vegetation gives scant cover for mice or voles that venture onto the marsh and the Kestrels' success rate when hunting here seems high. Buzzards *Buteo buteo* are also seen high overhead throughout the year but the saltmarsh seems to hold no great attraction for them.

Another year-round visitor is the Peregrine *Falco peregrinus*. Nesting on not-too-distant cliffs, they are most often seen hunting across the saltmarshes in winter time when they make the most of the large number of weary waders and wildfowl that drop into the saltmarshes to rest or feed.

During the winter months Merlin *Falco columbarius* are quite frequent visitors to the saltmarshes. These birds may come from Scandinavia, Iceland, from upland areas of the UK and possibly from Exmoor where they have bred for many years but now seem to be in something of a decline.

The large numbers of wintering Meadow Pipits and Wagtails are their most regularly targeted prey species when hunting.

Although the numbers of wintering Short-eared Owls *Asio flammeus* are not high across Somerset, these saltmarsh areas with their low, sparse, vegetation are a likely place to find them. They may have travelled to Somerset from countries such as France, Belgium, Sweden, Finland, Russia or Iceland.

When flying low over the marshes in the late afternoon, often in very good light, they appear to have an effortless way of flying, almost as if they are moving in slow-motion. They can appear on the marshes at almost any time between October and April. Although voles are their favourite prey they also take rats and small rabbits, and on the saltmarshes Pipits, Skylarks and Wagtails are likely to form a large part of their diet.

Mammals

Few land mammals find the coast an agreeable place to live. Birds can cope with an unexpected influx of sea water; they just open their wings and fly away. The drier, landward side of the saltmarshes are where mice and voles can find ground high enough in which to burrow, but many of these areas are periodically overcome by the sea and small mammals will be drowned.

Rabbits *Oryctolagus cunniculus* are the most common mammal seen across the marshes. Many of these do not burrow but live in dense, scrubby thickets found along the various earthbank seawalls that surround marshes along the coast. Brown Hares *Lepus capensis* are very occasionally seen out on the saltmarsh and also seem comfortable moving through some of the drier reed beds that border the marsh. Hares are much commoner on the drier grazing land behind many of these marsh areas. Roe Deer *Capreolus capreolus* are fairly common in fields behind the marshes and make occasional forays onto the saltmarsh. Foxes *Vulpes vulpes*, Stoats *Mustela ermine* and Weasels *Mustela nivalis* all make periodic trips out onto the saltmarsh looking for prey. The largest land predator in the UK, the Otter *Lutra lutra* also makes occasional visits out onto the saltmarsh. Otters occur on many of the Somerset rivers and streams that feed into the fresh water and salt water marshes that lie along much of this coast.

6

Cliffs and Cliff Tops

Greater Black-backed Gulls *Larus marinus* and juvenile Herring Gulls *Larus argentatus*, Gore Point, May.

RIGHT, TOP TO BOTTOM
Peregrine *Falco peregrinus*,
seen along all the Somerset cliffs.

White Rock-rose *Helianthemum apenninum*, Brean Down.
A scarce native plant only found in Somerset and Devon.

Lichen *Ochrolechia parella*, Hurlstone Point.

Common Restharrow *Ononis repens*, Kilve cliff tops.

Small Heath *Coenonympha pamphilus*
occurs on many of Somerset's grassy cliff tops.

Cliffs form the backdrop to Somerset's beaches for 38 km, just over half of the coast's length of 73 km.

Somerset's longest continuous cliff section runs for 19.5 km from Blue Anchor Bay to Hinkley Point. These are the Somerset coast's lower cliffs. They vary enormously in height but fall roughly into the 10 to 40 metre height range. The low height of these cliffs, coupled with the fact that the land above them is relatively flat, accounts for the farming activities that take place only a short distance away from the cliff edge for much of their length.

The layers of Jurassic and Triassic rock, mudstones and shales that form these cliffs are quite soft. The higher tides break against them for much of the year and erosion by the sea is persistent with rockfalls, large and small, taking place all year round.

The considerably higher cliffs found at the east and west boundaries of Somerset are very different from the lower cliffs and also very different from each other.

On Somerset's eastern boundary the narrow peninsula of Brean Down juts out from the coast for 2.5 km. Surrounded by flat land behind and on either side, it has a dramatic, somewhat brooding presence in this otherwise low, sandy landscape.

The Down reaches close to 100 metres at its highest point with very sheer cliff faces on its southern side. Brean Down is a westerly extension of the Mendip Hills and is made from the same hard, Carboniferous Limestone that forms those hills as well as the spectacular Cheddar Gorge.

The Exmoor sea cliffs start at Minehead and to a large degree are inaccessible to human visitors, as are the beaches that lie in front of them. These cliffs, which are dramatically high and rugged, are of Old Red Sandstone and their lack of access is not surprising. Exmoor, the larger part of which lies in Somerset, has the highest coastline in England and Wales. Culbone Hill, which is 433 metres high, lies just west of Porlock Weir, and the highest sheer sea cliff in England and Wales is the 244-metre drop at Great Hangman at the Devon end of the Exmoor coast.

The Somerset Exmoor cliffs extend for a total of 14 km with Porlock's shingle beach breaking them into two parts.

BREAN DOWN

Brean Down has cliffs that extend around its perimeter for 4.5 km. Its seaward tip is occupied by Brean Fort which was built in response to fears of a French naval invasion and completed in 1870. The northern side, facing Weston-Super-Mare shelves down gently towards the sea with very low cliffs along much of its length. The southern side has high, vertical cliffs with some of the clifftop paths on this side passing dizzyingly close to the edge which is mostly unfenced.

The Down has been owned by the National Trust since 1952. The Trust manages the grassland that covers much of the higher slopes by grazing it with a combination of White Park cattle during the summer months, and some 50 breeding goats throughout the year. Although the livestock maintains the flower-rich grassland here in good condition, the grazing pressure is not enough to stop scrub and Bracken *Pteridium aquilinum* from seeding and spreading across the grassland. National Trust staff and volunteer teams hold regular winter work parties here to cut back the scrub and clear Bracken that has encroached onto the grassland.

Although the village of Brean itself has been subjected to intense holiday development the Down remains largely impervious to the bustle below.

Limestone grassland

Brean Down is justifiably famous for the plant-rich Limestone grassland that occurs along the top of the Down and on its rocky, southern slopes. During the summer months this is spectacular place to visit, alive with flowers and the beetles, bugs, weevils and butterflies that depend upon them.

The predominantly short, grassy sward on the top of the Down is dominated by several species of fine Fescue grasses including Red Fescue *Festuca*

Cliffs west of Kilve, an important site for cliff top grassland plants.

Brean Down, May, Bluebells *Hyacinthoides non-scripta* and Hawthorn *Crataegus monogyna*.

The final section of the steep and very narrow path onto Glenthorne beach.

rubra, Sheep's-fescue *Festuca ovina* and Tall Fescue *Festuca arundinacea*. Among these grasses grow Salad Burnet *Sanguisorba minor*, Yellow-wort *Blackstonia perfoliata*, Common Centaury *Centaurium erythraea*, Small Scabious *Scabiosa columbaria*, Fairy Flax *Linum catharticum*, and Wild Carrot *Daucus carota*.

In addition, rocky-coast plants like Thrift *Armeria maritima*, Sea Campion *Silene uniflora*, Buck's-horn Plantain *Plantago coronopus* and Danish Scurvy-grass *Cochlearia danica* creep up onto the Down and mix with the limestone grassland plants, adding greatly to the diversity of plant life here.

The southern slopes of the Down give wonderful, often hazy blue, views across to the Quantocks and Exmoor, 20 and 30 km away respectively. On this slope is a unique community of nationally rare species of plants. Two of these are listed in the British Plant Red Data Book: Somerset Grass *Koeleria vallesiana* is a species found in Britain only on Brean Down and on a few south-facing slopes in the Mendips, and White Rock-rose *Helianthemum apenninum* is found only on coastal limestone grasslands in Somerset and Devon. The very local Dwarf Sedge *Carex humilis* also occurs here, flowering in March and April, and is usually the earliest sedge to flower.

The bright yellow Goldilocks Aster *Aster linosyris* also occurs on Brean Down, mainly on grassy ledges on the southern cliff face and only in small numbers. This is a perennial plant which is found at only a handful of sites in the UK. It flowers late in the year, the best time to find it being between September and November.

There are several places on the southern slopes of the Down where Ivy *Hedera helix* scrambles over the exposed Limestone rocks. Growing with it is Ivy Broomrape *Orobanche hederae*, which is parasitic on Ivy but only on subspecies *hibernica*. It has a south-west distribution and is more at home growing on rocks and walls than on trees.

Three species of orchid have been found on the Down: the spring-flowering Green-winged Orchid *Orchis morio*, Bee Orchid *Ophrys apifera* flowering in May and June and Autumn Lady's-tresses *Spiranthes spiralis* flowering around September time.

Butterflies

The great variety of plants on the Down make this a very attractive site to many insects including butterflies Twenty-six species have been recorded here including Small Skipper *Thymelicus sylvestris*, Small Copper *Lycaena phlaeas*, Brown Argus *Aricia agestis*, Common Blue *Polyommatus icarus*, Chalkhill Blue *Lysandra coridon*, Dark Green Fritillary *Masoacidalia aglaja*, Marbled White *Melanargia galathea* and Grayling *Hipparchia semele*.

The Grayling is not confined to coastal habitats but is certainly the butterfly that seems most at home in bare, sandy or rocky terrain, as here, high up on the Down. The Graylings' flight and landing technique makes it perfectly adapted to escape detection in such habitats. When settling to rest on bare ground or rock, its habit of rapidly closing its wings and then leaning body and wings sideways until almost flat on the ground, combined with the camouflage of its mottled grey underwing, means it is instantly lost to sight.

Brean microclimates

During the summer months the cliff tops at Brean Down offer the chance to experience a remarkable range of coastal microclimates and see their effect on habitat here. By the first days of July much of the grassland across the top of the Down and also on the south-facing slopes may be withered and straw coloured. This is caused by a combination of predominantly south-westerly winds drying out soil and plants very effectively, as well as intense solar radiation. At the same time the north-facing slope, which looks towards Weston-Super-Mare, faces away from the sun and is well sheltered from the south-westerly winds, remains covered in lush green vegetation.

Brean's north-facing slopes

The north-facing slopes of the Down are considerably less precipitous than the south-facing cliffs. This is a much more gentle and well-vegetated landscape. These slopes do lead down to cliffs but they are mostly only a few metres high and are an excellent place to sit and watch the tides as they sweep across the sand below you.

Much of this north-facing slope has a thick covering of grass and scrubby vegetation comprising species such as

◄ **White Rock-rose** *Helianthemum apenninum*, **Brean Down, May**, one of Somerset's scarcest plants but abundant at this site.

Ivy Broomrape *Orobanche hederae*, **Brean Down**, very much a coastal species in Somerset. ▶

Brown Argus *Aricia agestis*, **Brean Down**, despite its colour it is a member of the 'Blue' family of butterflies. ▶

Grayling *Hipparchia semele*, **Brean Down**, a butterfly of bare rocky ground and other dry open habitats such as dunes. ▶

Brambles *Rubus fruticosus*, Wild Privet *Ligustrum vulgare* and Elder *Sambucus nigra*. Bracken also occurs in considerable quantity on this slope. Small Hawthorn trees *Crataegus monogyna* are to be found right across this landscape. Many of these Hawthorns are scattered, isolated trees while others cluster in dense groups. Hawthorn is known to be somewhat tolerant of salt-spray conditions and this appears to account for it being the 'climax woodland' that has developed on Brean Down.

Vegetation grows most densely on the lower slopes, where the soil is thicker. Here, among the brambles and Bracken can be found Hedge Bedstraw *Gallium mollugo*, Black Bryony *Tamus communis*, Slender Thistle *Carduus tenuiflorus* and, surprisingly for such a dry landscape, Marsh Thistle *Circium palustre*. Higher up the slopes where the soil is thinner and the turf much shorter, Dropwort *Filipendula vulgaris*, Kidney Vetch *Anthyllis vulneraria*, Common Bird's-foot-trefoil *Lotus corniculatus* and Bird's-foot Clover, also known as Fenugreek *Trifolium ornithopodiodes*, can all be found.

In the summer months the dense Bracken and Bramble that cover much of these slopes provide ideal nesting habitats for Dunnock *Prunella modularis*, Long-tailed Tit *Aegithalos caudatus*, Robin *Erithacus rubecula* and Stonechat *Saxicola torquata*. All these birds are resident on Brean Down but they are also joined each year by several pairs of the summer-visiting

Whitethroat *Sylvia communis* which find the low, wind-sculpted scrub here much to their liking as a place to nest.

A more surprising bird visitor to Brean Down in recent times has been our rarest member of the Crow family, the Chough *Pyrrachorax pyrrachorax*. Five birds appeared in March 2007 and stayed for several days, following the appearance of a single Chough in north Somerset in 2006. These birds were ringed and subsequently identified as birds that came from the Welsh Chough population.

Records show that Choughs last bred in Somerset on cliffs west of Minehead in the late 1860s. The Hood Arms pub at Kilve has a Chough and anchor on its sign, a strong indication that Choughs were once present along this part of the coast. The pub was in fact called the Chough and Anchor from 1689 until 1832 when it took on its modern name.

The Welsh Chough population has expanded considerably in recent years and this has led to Choughs exploring for new nesting sites further afield. In 2002 a pair of Choughs bred in Cornwall on the Lizard Peninsula. This was the first time in over 50 years that Choughs had bred in England, the last pair having bred in Cornwall in 1947.

Choughs disappeared in England as breeding birds mainly due to the loss of clifftop grasslands where they like to hunt for a wide variety of invertebrate life. Many semi-natural, plant- and insect-rich clifftop grasslands disappeared in the 1930s and '40s when they were ploughed up to grow

crops. Other clifftop grasslands were lost at about the same time when they were abandoned by farmers who felt it was uneconomic and unsafe to graze valuable livestock in such dangerous places. As a result these areas became invaded by scrub.

The Choughs' decline was compounded by the fact that as they became rarer taxidermists and egg collectors hunted down the last few remaining birds. It is quite possible that Choughs could return to breed in Somerset and not just to Brean Down. The Down has excellent insect-rich grasslands for them to feed on as well as good nesting sites in the rock crevices and mini caves high up on its steep, southern cliffs. There are other sites along this coast that could provide suitable habitat.

The Jackdaw *Corvus monedula* is the most abundant member of the crow family found on Brean Down, and is resident here throughout the year. Jackdaws nest in cracks and holes in the cliff faces and are supremely able and acrobatic flyers, completely at home in the immensely strong winds that come off the sea to buffet the Down. Ravens *Corvus corax* are also masters of the air and can be seen on and over the Down throughout the year. They also nest on ledges on the steeper cliffs here.

Migration stop-off point
Many birds that migrate in spring and autumn follow coastlines as part of their navigation strategies and Brean

Whitethroat *Sylvia communis* **on Hawthorn** *Crataegus monogyna,* **Brean Down,** the dense scrub on the northern side provides ideal nesting and feeding habitat.

Chough *Pyrrhocorax pyrrhocorax* last bred in Somerset late 1860s but several have turned up on Brean Down in recent years. They have recently started to breed in Cornwall.

Common Centaury *Centaurium erythraea,* **Brean Down, July,** a member of the Gentian family

Down's prominence on this coast is likely to make it a well-known migration feature to passing birds. Its position and height also seem to make it an appealing stop-off point for tired, long-distance flyers. Every year in spring and autumn large numbers of birds, often in their hundreds, land on the Down to rest a while before resuming their marathon journeys. These include Meadow Pipit *Anthus petrosus*, Yellow Wagtail *Motacilla flava*, Barn Swallow *Hirundo rustica* and House Martin *Delichon urbica*. Other migrant bird species that appear regularly, but much fewer in number, include Hobby *Falco subbuteo*, Merlin *Falco columbarius*, Ring Ouzel *Turdus torquatus* and Whinchat *Saxicola rubetra*.

The Wheatear *Oenanthe oenanthe* is another migrant bird that regularly stops-off on Brean Down during migration time. Two 'races' of Wheatear appear on Somerset's coast; birds that breed in Greenland, Iceland and north-east Canada are subspecies *leucorha* and are larger and darker birds than those that nest in the UK and Europe. Both 'types' of Wheatear may drop in on Brean Down, and along other parts of this coast as they make their way to and from their wintering grounds in Africa. A very few Wheatear breed at the western end of the Somerset coast.

Brean's southern cliffs

It is well worth crossing the boulder beach to view the lower faces of the mostly sheer, Limestone cliffs on the south side of Brean. However,

it is a very rough and slippery place and great care needs to be taken to ensure that you are not caught out by a fast, incoming tide.

Many of the vertical cliff faces here are covered to a large extent with orange, yellow and black lichens. Lichens are fungi that have an algae living within them. The algae carries out photosynthesis and produces sugars which are used by it and the fungi as food. Many lichens have complex and attractive forms when viewed close up, but they can also be very hard to identify without specialist knowledge.

The black lichens that look like tar deposited on the rocks occur low down on the cliff and also on rocks that are regularly washed over by the higher tides. The most common of these is the Black Tar Lichen *Verrucaria maura*. These areas of black lichens often have smaller patches of white lichens among them that are likely to be *Ochrolechia parella*. The yellow or orange lichens tend to occur higher up the cliffs and can be found in bands that may stretch for hundreds of metres. They will include species such as *Caloplaca marina*, *Caloplaca thallincola* and *Xanthoria parietina*.

Although Brean Down shares the same Carboniferous Limestone as the Mendips it does not have caves cutting deep through its interior as they do. Along this southern cliff there are just a few shallow sea caves that are reached by the higher tides. Although not deep or wet enough for significant populations of marine wildlife

to take up residence in them, one or two do have interiors that are encrusted with a mat-forming marine algae that is found more commonly on rocks in the intertidal area. *Rhodochortom purpureum* is a pinky-purple, velvet-like algae that has covered several square metres at the back of one cave. These particular encrusting algae must be a considerable age taking into account the large size of these patches and the extreme dryness they must endure during low tides in the summer months which must slow their growth rate considerably.

Immediately at the bottom of the cliff face there are places where rocks that have fallen have lodged, creating ledges where sandy soil has accumulated. In these shallow soils plants such as Rock Samphire *Crithmum maritimum*, Wild Carrot, Greater Knapweed *Centaurea nigra*, Common Restharrow *Ononis repens*, Lady's Bedstraw *Galium verum* and Sea Campion live a precarious existence only a very short distance above the reach of the higher tides.

These same accumulations of rock provide good nesting cavities for Rock Pipits which occur in quite high numbers along this beach. When walking on the beach below these cliffs both Kestels *Falco tinnunculus* and Peregrines *Falco peregrinus* are likely to appear suddenly, moving very fast overhead. Both of these birds-of-prey are found here throughout the year with these cliffs providing a good selection of high, and well hidden, nesting ledges on which to raise their young.

Wild Carrot *Daucus carota* **and the yellow Lady's Bedstraw** *Galium verum*, **Brean Down**, just above the high tide line on the southern cliffs.

The encrusting alga (seaweed) *Rhodochorton purpureum*, **Brean Down.** This velvet-like alga occurs in sea caves that are periodically washed by high tides.

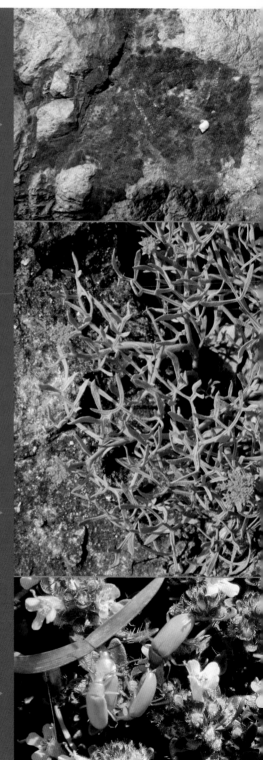

Rock Samphire *Crithmum maritimum*, **Brean Down**, occurs on the lower sea-splashed cliffs.

Sulphur Beetles *Cteniopus sulphureus* on Wild Thyme *Thymus polytrichus*, **Brean Down, July.**

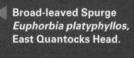

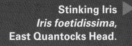

◄ Blackthorn *Prunus spinosa* hedge on cliff top **East Quantocks Head**, an important nectar source in the early part of the year.

◄ Bee Orchid *Ophrys apifera*, cliff top grassland, Shurton bars.

◄ Broad-leaved Spurge *Euphorbia platyphyllos*, East Quantocks Head.

Stinking Iris ►
Iris foetidissima, East Quantocks Head.

THE LOWER CLIFFS

Hinkley Point to Quantocks Head

Between Hinkley Point and Quantocks Head a public footpath runs along the top of the cliffs, giving spectacular views down to the intricate swirling patterns of the folded and wave-eroded Jurassic Limestone formations that form the beach here.

The islands of Steep Holm and Flat Holm can both be seen clearly from these cliffs, and across the sea Barry is the large town that faces this part of the Somerset coast. On clear winter days it is often possible to catch a glimpse of the snow-clad Brecon Beacons which lie some 80 km due north.

Although both crop- and livestock farming pushes close to the cliff edge along much of this path, there is still space for wildlife to thrive. Along considerable stretches there are narrow belts of low, shrubby vegetation between the coast path and the cliff edge that vary in width between one and three metres. These belts of scrub are kept well-pruned by the wind and salt spray and are composed of species such as Blackthorn *Prunus spinosa*, Hawthorn, Elder, Bramble and several species of wild Rose *Rosa* sp.

The dense impenetrability of these 'hedges' coupled with the fact that one side is unapproachable because it hangs over the cliff makes these very attractive, and safe, places for several species of bird to breed. Whitethroat,

Lesser Whitethroat *Sylvia curruca*, Yellowhammer *Emberiza citrinella*, Stonechat, Dunnock and Linnet *Carduelis cannabina* will all be found raising young here during the summer months.

During April and early May migrating Whinchats often put in a brief appearance on these clifftop bushes before making their way inland and west to nest in small numbers on the Quantocks and Exmoor. These clifftop areas of scrub are also well used by Wrens *Troglodytes troglodytes*. Some Wrens may nest low in the dense vegetation on the cliff top, but most tend to build their dome-shaped nests in the large cracks and crevices that are common in the crumbling cliff tops here, thus living up to their Latin name *Troglodyte* which means 'cave dweller'.

The Blue Lias Limestone rock from which many of the cliffs along this section are formed has a strong influence on the plant life found on the cliff tops. It gives rise to a plant-rich flora of a chalk/limestone, grassland type. This path has some wonderfully flowery areas with Agrimony *Agrimonia eupatoria*, Common Restharrow, Lady's Bedstraw, Wild Carrot, Pyramidal Orchid *Anacamptis pyramidalis* and Bee Orchid.

At Quantocks Head the public footpath turns inland towards the village of East Quantoxhead. This path leads between arable fields where Broad-leaved Spurge *Euphorbia platyphyllos* has something of a stronghold. Broad-leaved

Spurge is very much a plant of arable fields and disturbed ground. It is very thinly spread across Somerset and this is the only site where it occurs close to the coast.

Watchet to Blue Anchor

The coast path between Blue Anchor and Watchet runs alongside and through several areas of broadleaf woodland that form a narrow belt along much of the cliffs here, as well as literally 'tumbling' down the cliff face. The woodlands here are formed from a diverse mix of trees including Beech *Fagus sylvatica*, Ash *Fraxinus excelsior*, Oak *Quercus robur*, Hazel *Corylus avellana* and Sycamore *Acer pseudoplatanus*.

These woodlands sit right on the cliff edge where it is often very windy and the ground rather dry. Consequently many of the trees that grow here are rather stunted and the summer leaf canopy is light, allowing a dense woodland ground flora to develop.

The low-growing Dog's Mercury *Mercurialis perennis* grows thickly here and covers large areas. Wild Privet, Ivy and Honeysuckle *Lonicera periclymenum* creep over much of the ground but there is plenty of space for other plants like Bugle *Ajuga reptans*, Black Bryony, Stinking Iris *Iris foetidus*, Hart's-tongue Fern *Phyllitis scolopendrium* and the small, evergreen shrub Spurge-laurel *Daphne laureola*. This scarce, native shrub flowers very early in the year here on the coast, often in January and

February, and has pale green, trumpet-like flowers followed by black berries.

During May and June three species of orchid grow in these woodlands: Common-spotted Orchid *Dactylorhiza fuchsia*, the easy-to-overlook and green-flowered Common Twayblade *Listera ovata* and Bird's-nest Orchid *Neottia nidus-avis*. The latter has no chlorophyll and is consequently a rather dull brown colour even when it is very much alive and in full flower. All orchids, and many other plants too, have what are known as mychorrizal fungi in their root systems. The relationship between the fungi and their host is described as 'symbiotic'; the fungi, which are threadlike and not

Bird's-nest Orchid *Neottia nidus-avis* in cliff top woodland near Blue Anchor and Watchet, also occurs in woodland at Porlock Weir.

particularly robust, gain a 'body' by living in the orchid's roots, and the orchid feeds on organic nutrients that the fungi draw out of the soils.

Most orchids also have chlorophyll and photo-synthesise in order to create their own sugars, as well as making use of the nutrients provided by the fungi. In the case of the Bird's-nest Orchid, however, it has abandoned photosynthesis and relies entirely on the mychorrizal fungi to provide it with nourishment. It is called 'Bird's-nest' because the root system roughly resembles the woven twig-nest of a Blackbird *Turdus merula* or Thrush.

These clifftop woodlands are well populated with resident Blackbirds, Song Thrushes *Turdus philomelos*, Great Tits *Parus major*, Blue Tits *Parus caeruleus* and Long-tailed Tits as well as the summer-visiting warblers Chiffchaff *Phylloscopus collybita*, Willow Warbler *Phylloscopus trochilus* and Blackcap *Sylvia atricapilla*.

Just to the east of Blue Anchor Bay the coast footpath takes you to a part of these woods that has been much affected by the power of the sea. There has been a spectacular landslip here and mature trees such as Oak and Sycamore *Acer pseudoplatanus* are gently sliding towards the beach on islands of vegetation that are only held together by their roots.

There are great rents in the ground a metre or so deep where tree roots are exposed and stretched taut. Trees stand and lie at all kinds of angles, reminiscent of an earthquake

zone. Common-spotted Orchids and Bird's-nest Orchids continue to grow here, impervious to the havoc around them. The dried stems and seed heads of last year's orchid plants give an air of permanence to the woodland, seemingly unconcerned by its slow toboggan ride down towards the sea.

This woodland is the natural climax vegetation that has developed over hundreds, if not thousands, of years on this part of the coast. It provides the long-term, sheltered and stable woodland habitat that many woodland plants and animals require if they are to colonise initially and then thrive in a woodland.

The erosion by the sea of the cliffs that has taken place here, and led to the collapse of the wooded upper part of the cliffs, is a natural part of coastal landscape activity. The tragedy here is not so much the collapse of the wood into the sea, but the fact that cultivation of crops is taking place right up to the edge of the very narrow strip of woodland that remains on the flat top of the cliff. If given space this woodland has a natural capacity to regenerate itself, to grow and spread on the flat land that lies behind it. Although many woodland plants are slow to colonise new woodland areas, if given time they will spread and thrive. Perhaps future strategic, landscape-scale conservation plans will give this woodland and the community of plants and animals that have evolved in this unique coastal strip the space to prosper into the future.

Great Tit *Parus major*, **cliff top woodland Glenthorne**, there are many natural cavities to nest in in the dead or dying trees on the unstable cliff tops here.

Blue Tit *Cyanistes caeruleus*, found in all the cliff top woodlands along Somerset's coast.

Song Thrush *Turdus philomelos* occurs in many of Somerset's coastal woodlands.

Blackcap *Sylvia atricapilla* breeds in scrub and woodland all along the Somerset coast.

EXMOOR CLIFFS AND CLIFF TOPS

Exmoor National Park starts just west of Minehead and Somerset's coast remains in the National Park right up to the Somerset-Devon boundary on the coast at Glenthorne.

The coast path west from Minehead is also the formal start to the 'South West Coast path'. Due to the very rugged nature of this section of coast the official coast path is set a considerable way back from the cliffs and beaches, and at some points it is around 1 km inland. There is an 'unofficial', signposted alternative coast path that runs closer to the coast and roughly parallel with the formal path for some 6 km which allows even more spectacular views down the steep grass slopes and rocky cliff tops to the sea below. This is, however, as the signposts point out, a very rugged and narrow track that travels precipitously up and down as it drops into and climbs out off the steep valleys that lead down to the sea.

This 'rugged' path runs above the areas known as the Eastern and Western Brockholes. These names refer to the fact that these steep slopes, covered in Bramble and Bracken, have provided the ultimate in secluded hideaways for Badgers *Meles meles* to establish their setts for many years.

A kilometre or so to the east of Hurlstone Point the 'rugged path' cuts across the top of East Combe and Henners Combe. They can look like possible routes down to Selworthy Sands which are a tempting sight when they are

exposed at low tide. The reality, however, is that head-high brambles and scrub make an almost impenetrable barrier as you near the bottom of these valleys. In addition, the lower slopes are very unstable here with regular cliff falls taking large areas of scrub and grass with them crashing down onto the beach. It is best to keep well clear of these areas and leave them to the wildlife that have so few places they can call their own these days. Looking down from high up on the path is the best way to enjoy this section of the coast, leaving the Badgers, Stonechats, Whinchats, Meadow Pipits, Rock Pipits, Wrens, Ravens and Peregrines to their own devices.

This is one of the quietest sections of the Somerset coast, relatively undisturbed by visitors. It is in fact one of the best untouched areas—almost wilderness—that we have left anywhere in the south-west of England.

Whether taking the main Coast Path or the 'rugged path' between Minehead and Hurlstone Point, a walk of about 5 km, these coastal hills give the most outstanding views out across the Severn Sea and towards Wales. The 308-metre-high Selworthy Beacon, which lies above the villages of Selworthy and Bossington, provides spectacular views to east and west of just about the whole of the Somerset coast.

Maritime heath

As well as allowing tremendous views across the sea this

section of the coast path also takes you through a particular type of vegetation known as Maritime heath. Maritime heaths occur only very close to the sea and only in the south-west peninsula and in South Wales.

The importance of this habitat, both locally and nationally, is recognised by its European designation as the Exmoor Coastal Heath's Special Area of Conservation or SAC. Maritime heaths differ from upland heathland as found on Scottish hills, and from heathlands that occur well inland on lower ground, in the types of low-growing shrubs that comprise the heath.

What makes Maritime heath special is that it is dominated by a mixture of Western Gorse *Ulex gallii,* Bell Heather *Erica cinerea,* Heather *Calluna vulgaris* and the tussock-forming grass Bristle Bent *Agrostis curtisii.* Both Western Gorse and Bristle Bent are found almost exclusively on the west side of the UK.

The somewhat larger Common Gorse *Ulex europaeus,* which does occur, dotted about on these heaths, can flower throughout the year but is often at its best between April and June. Western Gorse, however, flowers between July and October, the same time as the heathers, which can often give rise to spectacular yellow and purple clifftops in late summer. Other major constituents of the heathland here are Bilberry *Vaccinium myrtillus,* and where the ground is damper, Cross-leaved Heath *Erica tetralix.*

◀ **Western Brockholes from Bossington Hill.**

The very unstable, rocky, scree slopes just east of Hurlstone Point. ▶

Open grassland on path down to Glenthorne, home to the Green Hairstreak *Callophrys rubi* and many other butterflies. ▶

The parasitic Dodder *Cuscuta epithymum* can often be seen here covering the low heath vegetation with its dense network of dark red threads. Dodder has no functioning leaves and relies on obtaining nourishment by tapping into the stems and roots of gorse and heather. It has tiny, pink-white flowers which can be seen from July to September. The Dodder itself is food for a very small and rare weevil, *Smicronyx jungermanniae* which is nationally scarce but has a strong population on these Somerset heaths.

An insect that is much easier to identify occurs quite commonly on paths through the heathland; the irridescent Green Tiger Beetle *Cicindela campestris*, which is a voracious predator on any small invertebrates it comes across. Green Tiger Beetles race across the bare ground at a speed that makes it hard to keep track of them but which is an ideal way to pounce on unsuspecting prey items.

In stark contrast to the Tiger Beetles' great speed are two other large black beetles, the Bloody-nosed Beetle *Timarcha tenebricosa* and the Minotaur Beetle *Typhaeus typhoeus*. They are often seen moving across these paths at a slow, lumbering pace, apparently oblivious to all around them.

Another slow-moving creature likely to be seen crossing these paths in late summer is the caterpillar of the Oak Eggar moth *Lasiocampa quercus*. This is a large caterpillar, up to 10 cm in length, that feeds mainly on heather and is very much restricted to heathland. The adult Oak Eggar moths are on the wing between May and September and the large brown male moths are unusual in regularly flying during the daytime.

Grayling butterflies are very much at home on these coastal heaths and can be seen on the wing here between June and September. Their caterpillars feed on grasses. Another butterfly frequently seen here is the Green Hairstreak *Callophrys rubi* whose caterpillars feed on Gorse and Bilberry. It is on the wing between April and July. Other more common butterflies found here include Meadow Brown *Maniola jurtina*, Small Heath *Coenonympha pamphilus*, Small Copper *Lycaena phlaeas* and Common Blue.

The mosaic of open ground and dense heath vegetation combined with the mild coastal climate make this ideal reptile habitat and Common Lizards *Zootoca vivipera* and Adders *Vipera berus* are regularly seen here. Both of these species have seen big declines in their numbers across the UK in recent years, but this part of the Somerset coast is very much a stronghold for them.

This heath habitat, and its abundance of insect life, is also highly attractive to three insectivorous birds that regularly nest here. Wheatears and Whinchats are both summer migrants that spend the winter in Africa and travel to this part of Somerset to raise their young, while Stonechats are resident throughout the year. Wheatears nest in holes in walls, in rabbit burrows and rock crevices, and the nearby boulder-strewn cliffs provide plenty of cavities for them to choose from. Both Whinchat and Stonechat nest close to the ground, often in dense grass tussocks or very low in gorse bushes. Whinchats are very much the scarcer of the two chats found here.

Dartford Warblers *Sylvia undata* have also bred on these clifftop heaths in recent years following a series of mild winters that allowed them to considerably increase their range in southern England. They were not known as a breeding bird in Somerset before 1980. Being a resident, insectivorous, warbler does pose problems though when winters are hard, and the very severe and snowy winters of 2009 and 2010 reduced the population considerably.

Rock and scree slopes east of Hurlstone Point

Immediately east of Hurlstone Point lies a landscape that is very different from much of Somerset's rather gentle coast. This is a harsh, stony hillside that slopes precipitously down to the shingle and boulder beach below.

High above the beach are steep, and very hard, Devonian, Hangman Grit sandstone cliffs from which large slabs of rock are being actively eroded by the elements. The biggest rockfalls take place mainly in winter when the thawing action of rain and frost can cause several square metres of cliff to come crashing down onto the jumbled boulders below. These rockfalls have created very substantial areas of loose and unstable scree that carpet many of the slopes here.

Maritime heathland high above the sea at North Hill west of Minehead, with Heather *Calluna vulgaris*, Bell Heather *Erica cinerea* and Western Gorse *Ulex galli*.

Oak Eggar moth *Lasiocampa quercus* **caterpillar, Bossington Hill.**

Green Hairstreak butterfly *Callophrys rubi* **on path down to Glenthorne.**

Heath Fritillary *Melltaea athalia*, one of Somerset's scarcest butterflies, occurs periodically on maritime heath west of Minehead.

This is a unique landscape, very raw and with very little opportunity for colonisation by vegetation. It closely resembles what much of the UK would have looked like after the last ice sheets retreated 10,000 to 12,000 years ago.

The freshly fallen rock is sharp and angular, but it will eventually make its way down onto the beach where it will be washed and rolled by the sea to become the smooth, rounded pebbles found on many Somerset beaches.

This part of Somerset's coast is a very harsh environment. It is particularly so during the winter when, due to the fact that the coast faces north and the hills behind block out most of the sun, many of these slopes sit in shadow even on the sunniest days. This, combined with the unstable nature of the scree, the steep slopes, and the crumbling cliffs falling to the beach below quickly make it apparent that this is not a place to venture into in a casual way.

This inaccessibility also makes it a wonderfully wild place. It is very much the haunt of Peregrines and Ravens whose harsh calls echo off the cliff faces as they swoop across the steep and rocky slopes, making the most of the strong winds and updrafts that blow here through much of the year.

Ravens and Peregrines tend to favour similar cliff ledges for their nesting places and in January and February there can be very noisy, aerial squabbles between these two species as they try to take possession of the same ledge.

Being able to finding safe and secluded nest sites on these and other Somerset cliffs has helped numbers of both these species to increase significantly in recent years. To many people these species are important indicators that the Somerset coast can still provide a home for two birds that are so symbolic of the wilder elements of Britain's countryside.

Despite being such an inhospitable environment, these steep, rocky scree slopes have their own specialised and hardy plant life which includes Navelwort *Umbilicus rupestris,* English Stonecrop *Sedum anglicum* and the ferns Black Spleenwort *Asplenium adiantum-nigrum,* Maidenhair Spleenwort *Asplenium trichomanes* and Polypody *Polypodium cambricum.* All these species are found throughout Somerset in man-made habitats such as dry-stone walls and old stone buildings, but this is where these species grew before man came on the scene. What can be seen here is in fact a slice of very ancient habitat.

Also growing on these cliffs, but only on those just above the spray of the sea, is another fern, Sea Spleenwort *Asplenium marinum,* which only grows on Somerset's cliffs westward from Minehead. Sea Spleenwort has shiny, green, rather leathery leaves which persist right through the winter.

The clean and moist sea air that blows across these scree slopes and the lack of competition from herbs and woody plants due to the stony and shifting nature of the terrain make this an ideal place for lichens to flourish. Many of the scree rocks and larger boulders are covered in an almost bewildering variety of lichens including *Lecanora atra, Ochrolechia parella, Rhizocarpon geographicum* and *Ramalina siliquosa,* known as Sea Ivory and one of the few lichens with a common name. Around 100 species of lichen can be found on the coastal heaths and rocks on this part of Somerset's coast.

Hurlstone Point

The path from Bossington out to Hurlstone Point not only leads to a breathtaking viewpoint but also gives very easy access to a mix of coastal rock and grassland plants that make this one of the best places to look for wildflowers in Somerset.

Much of the grassland here is dominated by Red Fescue grass which is pruned very short by rabbit grazing and the sea winds. Growing in the grassland next to the path and on rocks just above it you can see Thrift, Buck's-horn Plantain, Sea Campion, Rock Stonecrop *Sedum forsteranum,* Sea Stork's-bill *Erodium maritimum,* Upright Chickweed *Moenchia erecta,* Bluebell *Hyacinthoides non-scripta* and Early-purple Orchid *Orchis mascula.*

Two other plants which have a very limited distribution in the south of the UK are also found in this area. White Mullein *Verbascum lychnitis,* confusingly occurring in its yellow form in Somerset, also grows in the grassland. It does best where the grass is thin and the stony soil shows through, and is also found growing on stone walls. Cornish Moneywort *Sibthorpia europaea* occurs along stream edges and also in damp patches in the grassland, as well as along some of the damper tracks.

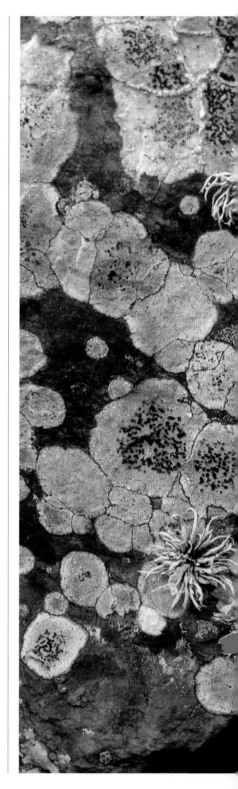

The bushy Sea Ivory lichen *Ramalina siliquosa* amongst others lichens, cliffs Hurlstone Point..

English Stonecrop *Sedum anglicum*, Hurlstone Point.

Sea Spleenwort *Asplenium marinum*, Hurlstone Point cliffs, restricted to a just a couple of sites along the coast.

Grassy heath habitat on route to Glenthorne beach. This sheltered valley has a mild microclimate that suites many invertebrate including the Small Pearl-bordered Fritillary *Boloria selene*.

Small Pearl-bordered Fritillary *Boloria selene* feeding on Greater Stitchwort *Stellaria holostea*, Glenthorne.

Dense Oak, Beech and Sycamore woodland just above the Glenthorne beach.

Treecreeper *Certhia familiaris*, a fairly common but easily overlooked bird in these western cliff edge woodlands.

Male Great Spotted Woodpecker *Dendrocopus major*. They may nest just a few metres back from the beach on these heavily wooded western cliffs.

Porlock Weir to Glenthorne

The 433-metre-high Culbone Hill lies 3 km west of Porlock and is the highest point along Somerset's coast. To put the height of this part of the coast into perspective, four Brean Downs stacked on top of one another do not quite reach to this height.

Although Culbone Hill gives great views out across the sea, the 6 km of cliffs that stretch from Porlock Weir to the county boundary at Glenthorne are completely hidden from view by the dense woodland that covers the slopes above the length of these cliffs.

The wooded slopes immediately above the cliffs are very steep and unstable, and there is no access to the cliffs or the beaches below them except from Porlock Weir or Glenthorne.

It is quite possible to walk west from Porlock Weir along the beach towards Gore Point and further too, but this is very rough terrain. The beach consists of very uneven shingle and boulders, and great care has to be taken to know exactly what the tides are doing, as many of the extra high spring tides come right up to the base of the cliffs making it very easy to be cut off. Rockfalls are also very much a feature of these cliffs and can occur at any time of year.

This lack of accessibility does, however, make it a very popular stretch of the coast to see seagulls. During the summer large flocks of gulls can be seen sitting around on many of the massive rocks that have crashed down from the cliffs. Many of these gulls will

be juvenile Herring Gulls *Larus argentatus*, born the previous year and not ready to breed until the following year. Juvenile Greater Black-backed *Larus marinus* and Lesser Black-backed Gulls *Larus fuscus* also sit out the summer here but in much smaller numbers than the Herring Gulls.

There are many well-hidden ledges along these cliffs and all three species, Greater Black-backed, Lesser Black-backed and Herring Gull, may find secure places to nest. The Greater Black-backed Gull is the least common of all the gulls found along the Somerset coast with a maximum of two to three pairs breeding at this very western end.

Oystercatchers *Haematopus ostralegus* are also found here throughout the year but there are only a handful, in great contrast to the many hundreds that winter at the other end of Somerset's coast. They nest in a wide range of sites, including on top of boulders at the back of the beach, and it is quite possible that there are suitable sites at several places along the base of these hard-to-visit cliffs.

Glenthorne, the most westerly beach and cliff in Somerset, can only be reached on foot. Getting to see this part of the coast requires a considerable amount of effort and the terrain is steep and rough. The final path onto the beach is often wet and slippery and runs through the narrow gorge that was cut by the stream that still runs beside it.

Glenthorne beach can be reached by a steep zig-zagging path that comes down from County Gate, a distance of about 2.5 km, or by deviating

from the South West Coast Path as it runs below Yenworthy Farm and Sugarloaf Hill.

The path down from County Gate passes through several areas of dense Hawthorn scrub which, during the summer months are alive with the sounds and activity of a wide range of birds that nest here. They include Whitethroat, Chiffchaff, Blackcap, Linnet, Stonechat, Blue Tit, Great Tit, Blackbird, Song Thrush, Bullfinch *Pyrrhula pyrrhula* and Yellowhammer.

At about the mid point of this path where the scrub thins out, the very sheltered grassy valley here is a good place to look out for some of the butterflies that can be found during the summer. Common Blue, Small Heath, Meadow Brown, Ringlet *Aphantopus hyperantus*, Dingy Skipper *Erynnis tages* and Grizzled Skipper *Pyrgus malvae* can all be seen flying in the summer months. This is also another very good place to see Green Hairstreaks which often occur here in large numbers.

The Small Pearl-bordered Fritillary *Boloria selene* is one of Somerset's rarest butterflies and only occurs on a handful of sites across the county. The rough grass with small patches of scrub on these steep slopes is very much to their liking and there is a strong colony here. Their caterpillars feed mainly on Common Dog-violet *Viola riviniana* which grows abundantly here and the adults are on the wing from late May until July.

The final section of the path passes through a wooded belt that lies just above the cliffs. This is likely to be another

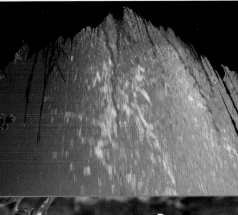

Glenthorne beach, behind the waterfall that marks the boundary between Somerset and Devon.

Silver Ragwort *Senecio cineraria*, introduced from the Mediterranean.

Nesting Fulmar *Fulmarus glacialis*, Glenthorne beach.

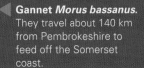

Gannet *Morus bassanus*. They travel about 140 km from Pembrokeshire to feed off the Somerset coast.

Fulmar in flight against Red Sandstone cliffs at Glenthorne beach.

distraction before reaching the beach and cliffs because it holds a good range of woodland birds including Great Spotted Woodpecker *Dendrocopus major* and Treecreeper *Certhia familiaris*.

The long trek down to Glenthorne is well worth the effort, part of the pleasure being the wonderful range of habitats that have to be passed through to get here.

The stream that the path follows on the last stretch to the beach is not the county boundary. This honour goes to the stream that passes through the garden of the adjacent, privately owned, Glenthorne House which lies on the Devon side of the stream. If for no other reason, it is worth the long slog down just to stand in front of the waterfall at the point where it splashes onto the beach.

The same access issues occur on Glenthorne beach as at the Porlock Weir end of these cliffs; this is a very rugged beach backed by steep cliffs that are washed by the higher tides. But that of course is their huge advantage as far as wildlife is concerned. The very low visitor numbers to this beach, and the feeling of remote tranquillity that can be experienced here, is in complete contrast to the bustle at the other end of Somerset's coast where access is easy. This is, of course, all part of the great diversity and attraction of this coast.

The Devonian Sandstone cliffs here are very buckled and shattered and there are many ledges and cracks that provide nesting and growing places. Although these cliff ledges

provide good places for native plants such as Sea Campion and Thrift to thrive, one of the most obvious cliff plants is Silver Ragwort *Senecio cineraria*, with its silver-grey foliage. This comes from the Mediterranean and was introduced into the UK as a garden plant before it escaped into the wild. There is no doubt that it is an attractive plant and it looks very much at home on rock ledges where it grows in its native Greece and Morocco. Its ability to thrive here is an indication of just how mild the climate can be on this coast. There is, however, a down side to non-native plants like this escaping into the wild; this plant will be preventing some of Somerset's natural cliff plants from prospering here.

Fortunately, another significant newcomer to the Glenthorne cliffs is a non-threatening and very welcome addition to Somerset's wildlife: the Fulmar *Fulmarus glacialis*.

Fulmars are members of the Petrel family which makes them more closely related to Albatrosses than to gulls. They are superb gliders, often travelling low over the sea on stiff wings that hardly seem to flap enough to keep them up in the air. This stiff-winged flight is often a good identification feature when they are seen from a distance.

They live much of their life far out at sea and will travel long distances to good feeding grounds. They pick up small fish on, and just under, the ocean's surface as well as zooplankton.

In the early 1900s Fulmars were restricted as breeding birds to remote islands such as St Kilda in Scotland. By the

1930s they had spread down through Scotland and then to coasts on both sides of England. They were first recorded breeding on the Exmoor coast, at the Devon end, in 1955 and only arrived as a breeding bird in Somerset on these cliffs in the late 1970s. Today four to six pairs breed at Glenthorne on a regular basis. Fulmars lay a single white egg on ledges that they have lined with plant material, and at this site Silver Ragwort is often the most convenient material to hand.

Fulmars are very long-lived; ringing and recovery projects have shown that they can live for up to 50 years.

Glenthorne is a very rewarding place to sit and look out to sea, to enjoy the effortless flight of the Fulmars, but also to see other seabirds that do not nest on this coast but regularly pass by. At about the same time as the Fulmars return to their nesting ledges in spring, Gannets *Morus bassanus* start to appear, feeding out in the Channel. Up to 20–30 birds may be seen together and sometimes quite close to the shore. They will have travelled here to feed from their colonies off the Welsh coast.

These cliffs also provide many well hidden nesting ledges for Herring Gulls, Lesser Black-backed and Greater Black-backed Gulls and all three species can be seen circling the cliffs here during the summer months.

Glenthorne's magnificent rugged cliffs create a spectacular western end to Somerset's coastline and are always worth visiting irrespective of the season.

APPENDIX 1
When you are at... look out for...

RIVER AXE

Lying immediately north of **Brean Down** and forming Somerset's boundary with North Somerset, the River Axe is worth visiting at any time of the year. The river banks can be reached by a footpath that lies below Brean Down on its south side.

During the winter it often has good numbers of wintering Teal, Wigeon, Lapwing and Redshank. Goosanders *Mergus merganser* also drop in here occasionally during the winter months. There are some good areas of saltmarsh here that often attract Curlew, Common Snipe and Little Egrets.

During the summer Meadow Pipits and Skylarks breed on the edge of the saltmarsh and Kestrels and Buzzards frequently hunt over the area.

BREAN DOWN

Part of the **Mendip Hills** and like them an exceptionally good place for wild flowers. Calcareous grassland plants found here include Autumn Gentian *Gentianella amarella*, Common Centuary and Yellow-wort. Bluebells *Hyacinthoides non-scriptus* and White Rock-rose make a dramatic display in spring and early summer.

The grassland on the top of the Down is also a good for butterflies including Grayling, Wall, Common Blue, Chalkhill Blue, Brown Argus and many commoner species.

During the summer many of the scrubby areas on the Down hold breeding Whitethroats. Stonechats also breed here occasionally.

Ravens and Peregrines nest on the cliffs as do good numbers of Jackdaws. The rocky beaches at the bottom of the cliffs are a particularly good place to see Rock Pipits, but you do have to be very careful about not being cut off by a fast rising tide.

BERROW

Berrow sand dunes which reach north to **Brean** and south to **Burnham** hold a wide range of plants that favour sand dunes or very dry ground, including Sea Spurge, Lyme Grass, Marram, Hound's-tongue, Bugloss, Great Mullein and Fragrant, Common and Small-flowered Evening-primroses. Sea-buckthorn also occurs commonly across the dunes.

In the damp dune slacks, landward of the dry dunes, there are areas of reedbed with a good range of marsh plants including Yellow Iris, Branched Bur-reed *Sparganium erectum*, Sea Club-rush and Southern Marsh-orchid. The reedbed and marsh areas have breeding Sedge Warblers, Reed Warblers, Reed Buntings and also a small colony of breeding Bearded Tits.

During the winter the berries on the Sea-buckthorn attract large numbers of Redwings and Fieldfares. Large numbers of Starlings also come to feed on the berries and then roost in the Sea-buckthorn bushes at night.

During the winter the sandflats are an important resting and feeding place for wintering and passage migrant waders, particularly for Dunlin, Sanderling, Ringed Plover and Knot. Oystercatchers also feed on the beach in large numbers during the winter.

Lying inland from the dunes is **Berrow Church**, and between the church and the road are some very plant-rich sandy meadows which have large numbers of Pyramidal Orchids and Common Spotted-orchids in May/June. Parts of this grassland are damp and here you can find Brookweed *Samolus valerandi* which is a scarce plant more often found on the Somerset Levels.

BURNHAM ON SEA

The 9 km stretch of sand dunes and sand flats that runs north from Burnham, is one of the longest continuous sand beaches in England. Walking north from Burnham up to **Brean** is a spectacular sand beach walk in winter or summer, and a local bus service can get you back to Burnham if that is where you are based.

In the summer months go north out of Burnham for sand dune flora including Sea Spurge, several species of Evening-primrose and Lyme Grass.

During the winter months waders such as Sanderling, Dunlin and Oystercatcher occur on the sand flats right in front of the town. This stretch of beach is also a good place to look out for Common Gulls during the winter.

There is good footpath access south out of Burnham and along the banks of the **River Brue**. The mouth of this river is a favourite haunt of Redshank, Ringed Plover, Curlew and Cormorants.

There are also areas of saltmarsh on the river banks and at the mouth of the Brue which are well used by waders and ducks in winter and summer. These saltmarsh areas are favourite feeding places for Little Egrets and Grey Herons. If you walk about 1.5 km upstream along the river footpath you can cross the Brue on a footbridge and then walk south to the **Huntspill River**. This is a man-made river constructed partly to help drain the Somerset levels. It is now the **Huntspill River National Nature Reserve** and is an excellent place to see breeding Shelduck during the summer and also Kingfishers *Alcedo atthis*, Great Crested Grebe *Podiceps cristatus* and Little Grebe *Tachybaptus ruficollis*. Barn Owls *Tyto alba* can often be seen hunting along the grassy banks of the river and Otters also hunt here.

COMBWICH

Combwich gives easy access to the footpath that runs alongside **River Parrett** as it heads towards the sea, and this path is also part of the **River Parrett Trail**. During winter very large numbers of waders, particularly Dunlin, come up the Parrett when the high tide pushes them off the mudflats. Redshank, Grey Plover, Knot and Black-tailed Godwit all occur regularly along the muddy banks of the Parrett and are easily seen from the footpath. Avocets also winter regularly along this part of the river. Wigeon, Teal and Shelduck also occur in good numbers. This riverside path goes all the way through to **Steart**. Peregrines, Kestrels and Buzzards can be seen hunting here throughout the year.

STEART

Steart is the access point for **Bridgwater Bay National Nature Reserve**. It is an area with many small grazing marsh fields and also saltmarsh. Several hides overlook the coast and saltmarsh but you will only see anything from them during high tide when birds feeding out on the mudflats are pushed up towards the hides. Very large numbers, often several thousand, of wintering Shelduck can be seen feeding out on the mudflats. There is an excellent tower hide giving spectacular views over this part of the coast. Curlew, Whimbrel, Knot, Dunlin, Ringed Plover, Golden Plover and Lapwing are amongst the waders that occur in large numbers here during the winter months. Peregrines and Merlin also hunt here a lot during the winter.

Yellow-wort, Brean Down

Great Mullein, Berrow Dunes

Slelduck, Huntspill River

Wigeon, River Parrett

Lapwing, Steart

There are several areas of reedbed with breeding Reed Bunting, Sedge Warbler and Reed Warbler. This is also a good place for Cuckoo's *Cuculus canorus* during the summer.

Just south of Steart lies the **Wall Common** saltmarsh area with Sea Spurge, Sea-lavender, Sea Wormwood and Glasswort.

STOLFORD

The shingle bank that runs east from Stolford has a diverse flora including Yellow Horned-poppy, Slender Thistle, Sea Mayweed, Sea Beet, Musk Stork's-bill, Biting Stonecrop and Wild Carrot.

The seaward side of this shingle bank is very much a favourite place for Turnstones during the winter and Curlew, Whimbrel, Grey Plover, Redshank and large numbers of Ostercatchers also congregate here. At high tide many of these birds move over onto the saltmarsh behind the shingle.

Large numbers of wintering Wigeon can be seen on the sea as well as small groups of Pintail and Brent Geese.

Wintering Short-eared Owl often turn up on the saltmarsh and Snow Buntings are also regular winter visitors.

Going west on the coast path from Stolford takes you to **Hinkley Point**. The power station buildings are a favourite place for Herring Gulls and Lesser Black-backed Gulls to nest and Black Redstarts *Phoenicurus ochruros* also regularly drop in here during spring and autumn migration time. This is the best place on the Somerset coast to look for Purple Sandpipers *Calidris maritima* which often come to winter on the rocky shore line in front of the power station.

Rock Sea-lavender *Limonium binervosum* grows on the concrete and boulder sea wall that defends this part of the coast.

LILSTOCK

Part of the shingle beach here has a steep densely wooded cliff habitat behind it giving a great combination of beach and woodland habitats. Treecreepers, Nuthatches and Great Spotted Woodpeckers are all resident and breed in this wood. During the summer Chiffchaffs and Willow Warblers also take up residence. Hart's-tongue Fern *Phyllitis scolopendrium* grows thickly on the almost vertical woodland floor.

Lilstock is good place to look for seaweeds at low tide and large numbers of Beadlet Anemones occur in the crevices in the Blue Lias rock platforms that are exposed a low tides.

KILVE

A stream that comes down from the Quantocks crosses the shingle beach at Kilve and a small freshwater pool occurs at the landward side of the shingle. This pool and the scrubby vegetation around it is a popular dropping-in place for migratory birds in spring and autumn. Swallow, House Martin, Sand Martin *Riparia riparia*, Chiffchaff, Willow Warbler and Cuckoo amongst many other species may be found here drinking or feeding on insects buzzing over the pool.

Kilve is also well known for the fossil Ammonites found on the beach.

Walking west along the cliff top path towards **East Quantocks Head** is a good way to experience the diverse flora that can be found here. Along with Alexanders you will find Wild Carrot, Salad Burnet, Common Bird's-foot-trefoil. Pyramidal Orchid and Bee Orchid both occur along this path and both flower end of May into June.

EAST QUANTOCKS HEAD

Like **Kilve**, East Quantocks Head is a well-known place to look for Ammonites and other fossils. The wave-cut platforms of Blue Lias are quite spectacular here, as are the layered and folded rocks that form the cliffs behind the shingle and rock beach.

Rock Pipits breed on the beach and Ravens and Peregrines periodically breed on the taller cliff sections.

The cliff top paths that go east and west from East Quantocks Head often have a thick Blackthorn scrub belt between the path and the cliff edge and this is a favourite place for Whitethroats, Linnets, Long-tailed Tits and Wrens to nest.

The path from the village of **East Quantoxhead** out to East Quantocks Head beach is very plant rich with Primrose *Primula vulgaris* in the spring, is also one of the few places in Somerset where you can see Broad-leaved Spurge.

DONNIFORD

Donniford has good rock pool life in the cracks and crevices of the Blue Lias rock platforms on the beach. Seaweeds are also diverse here.

The orange-red cliffs at the back of Donniford beach are relatively young, dating from the Pleistocene period, and the teeth and bones of mammoths have been found here along with the remains of other Ice Age animals.

WATCHET

Watchet Harbour is an excellent gull watching site with large numbers of Black-headed Gulls during the winter and

Herring Gulls throughout the year. The harbour walls are a good place to see Rock and Meadow Pipits during the winter and Pied Wagtails nest in several places around the harbour.

The rocky beach west of Watchet has many good rock pool areas and the cliffs here are quite spectacular.

The cliff top walk that goes east from Watchet towards **Doniford** is good for plants with lots of Alexanders, Wild Carrot and also the Garden Grape Hyacinth *Muscari armeniacum* which has become naturalised in these cliff top grasslands.

BLUE ANCHOR BAY

This is a busy beach during the summer but well worth visiting. You can walk west towards **Dunster Beach** along the beach, or the shingle bank at the back of the beach at any state of the tide. The shingle bank has a good flora including plants such as Weld and Tree Mallow.

Wintering Turnstone are often found along this beach and large numbers of Shelduck also feed in the shallows during the winter.

The cliffs to the east of Blue Anchor are some of the most spectacular anywhere in the south-west. They date from the Jurassic/Triassic period and are partly formed from white and pink Alabaster.

The cliffs here are eroding rather dramatically and the cliff top woodland is now crashing down onto the beach.

The cliff top path leading east out of Blue Anchor, and towards **Watchet**, takes you through this woodland which has a rich flora including Twayblade and Bird's-nest Orchids.

DUNSTER BEACH

This is one of the best places in Somerset for sand dune plants. Walking the sandy coast path towards **Minehead** is the best way to find many sand dune specialists including Sand Catchfly, Sea Clover, Fennel and Viper's Bugloss.

When the tide drops look out for Sand Mason Worms and Painted and Flat Top Shells.

During the winter Wigeon and Shelduck feed in the shallows and Oystercatcher and Curlew too. Sanderlings also regularly drop in to feed at low tide.

The **River Avill** crosses the beach at Dunster Beach and Otters come down this river very occasionally to forage on the beach. The chances of seeing them are very small but you might find their distinctive droppings (spraints), on large boulders in the stream.

Large numbers of gulls can congregate where the river enters the

Slender Thistle, Stolford

Pyramidal Orchid, Kilve

Rock Pipit, East Quantocks Head

Garden Grape Hyacinth, Watchet

Weld, Dunster Beach

sea to drink and wash in the fresh water and Mute Swans and Canada Geese also regularly gather here.

MINEHEAD

Minehead beach is a good place to look for marine life such as shells and seaweeds along the tidelines. At very low tides it is possible to find starfish on the newly exposed sands.

There is very good sand dune flora on the coast path going east from the seafront esplanade towards **Dunster Beach**. Prickly Saltwort occurs on the sand right in front of the town.

During winter, Oystercatchers, Curlew and other waders, come in to feed on the sand flats at low tide. Ringed Plovers often come to rest and feed on this beach during spring and autumn migration time.

The South West Coast Path starts in Minehead and walking west out of the town on this path soon brings you on to the wonderful open heathland high above the sea. As well as Heather, Bell Heather, Cross-leaved Heath, Western Gorse and Common Gorse you can find large areas turned a hazy red by the low growing Sheep's Sorrel *Rumex accetosella*. This area is also one of the best places in Somerset to see Common Dodder, a strange threadlike plant that is a parasite on Gorse and Heather.

Minehead Marshes lie immediately east of the town and south and east of Butlin's Holiday Camp. There is public access to a small part of this area, and the rest is grazed by livestock, but it can be looked over from the footpath that runs along Seaward Way which starts on the sea front, or from the footpath that runs from **Dunster Station** towards the sea.

Although much drier now than in the past, aerial views show a maze of old water channels that occurred in the marsh/saltmarsh that existed here before the Holiday Camp was built, Wigeon and Teal still come here in the winter and large numbers of Canada Geese drop in throughout the year.

HURLSTONE POINT

It is well worth climbing the path from **Bossington** up to Hurlstone Point just to get the panoramic view across **Porlock Marsh** and the shingle ridge. This is also an excellent place to watch over the sea looking out for passage migrant birds in spring and autumn. It is also a great place to sit in the summer to watch Herring Gulls, Lesser Black-backed and Greater Black-backed Gulls making expert use of the strong winds that blow up off the sea.

Gannets can often be seen fishing out in the channel during summer and Fulmars also regularly fly by. A very small number of summer visiting Wheatear occasionally breed in the jumble of rocks around Hurlstone Point. Rock and Meadow Pipits both breed here too. Hurlstone Point has an interesting flora including Thrift, Sea Stork's-bill and the very scarce Rock Sea-spurrey *Spergularia rupicola*, it is also an excellent place to see many of the lichen that grow so well along this coast.

PORLOCK

From Porlock you can visit both the massive coastal shingle bank and the saltmarsh that lies behind it. Several footpaths lead out from the town towards the sea. Porlock shingle bank has a great display of plants that are well adapted to this harsh environment including Yellow Horned-poppy, Sea Campion, Thrift and Sea Beet. Most plants occur on the landward side of the shingle where conditions are less harsh. This ridge is a good place to see Rock Pipits in summer, and in spring and autumn it is favourite haunt of migrating Wheatears.

The saltmarsh often has breeding Redshank and Shelduck and both species occur here in large numbers during the winter. Herons and Little Egrets are here throughout the year. During the summer Meadow Pipits and Skylarks breed round the drier edges of the marsh. Pied and Grey Wagtails also breed here.

Much of the wetter parts of the marsh are carpeted with Sea Purslane, whilst the drier parts have large areas of Sea Aster, Sea Milkwort and Greater Sea-spurrey.

PORLOCK WEIR

Porlock Weir lies at the western end of the vast **Porlock** shingle ridge and is a good place to set out to explore it. Here the shingle, which lies close to the small harbour, has a diverse flora including Tree Mallow, Sea Campion, Thrift, Sea Milkwort and Sea Beet and also many naturalised Mediterranean-type plants that have escaped from the cottage gardens that back onto the beach. Purple Toadflax, Red Valerian, Snapdragon and Wallflower can all be found growing happily on the shingle here.

Walking west from the harbour takes you to a very accessible area of saltmarsh with a good range of plants such as Sea Arrowgrass, Sea Plantain, Sea Club-rush and Sea Purslane which covers large areas of the saltmarsh.

Continuing along the shingle and rock beach will take you to **Gore Point**, about 1.5 km from the harbour, but you do have to know what the tide is doing to get there safely. This is a very good rockpool area at low tide with the chance of finding Edible, Porcelain and Hermit Crabs, Brittle Stars and much other marine life.

Worthy Wood which lies on the steep slopes immediately behind Porlock Weir is a fine area of ancient woodland with a rich flora including Bluebells and Bird's-nest Orchids. Footpaths go up through this wood from Porlock Weir.

Taking the South West Coast Path west out of Porlock Weir leads you up through **Yearnor Wood** which is too dense to allow views of the sea but provides great habitat for the summer visiting Pied Flycatchers *Ficedula hypoleuca*, Wood Warblers *Phylloscopus sibilatrix* and Redstarts *Phoenicarus phoenicarus* which all breed in these woods.

GLENTHORNE

This is the most westerly point of the Somerset coast. The stone and shingle beach here can only be reached by a steep footpath down from **County Gate** on the A39, or by deviating off of the South West Coast Path. The upper part of this path is open and grassy and is an excellent place to see Green Hairstreak and Small Pearl-bordered Fritillary butterflies during the summer.

The last part of this path is through a deep wooded valley that is partly ancient Oak woodland rich in flowering plants, ferns and lichens.

There is a waterfall onto the beach and it is this stream that forms the county boundary between Somerset and **Devon.**

This is the best place in Somerset to see passing seabirds such as Kittiwake *Rissa tridactyla*, Razorbill *Alca torda* and Guilemot *Uria aalge* which all nest a little further to the west in Devon. A small number of Fulmars nest on the cliffs here and they can be seen along this part of the coast throughout the year.

As well as finding Thrift and Sea Campion on the cliffs here you will see Silver Ragwort which is a plant native to southern Europe and that has only recently started to colonise these cliffs and others west into Devon.

Glenthorne is one of the very best places in Somerset to look for seaweeds and other marine life at low tide. But it is a very long walk down to the beach and then back up again!

Cross-leaved Heath, North Hill, Minehead

Dark Green Fritillary, Bossington

Henbane, Porlock Weir

Painted Goby in rock pool, Gore Point

Chiffchaff, Glenthorne

BEYOND SOMERSET

Wildlife is not concerned about county boundaries and there is some very fine coastal habitat either side of Somerset. Included here are several sites that occur in **North Somerset** and **Devon** to give an idea of what lies beyond Somerset's borders.

NORTH SOMERSET

Sand Point and Middle Hope

Just north of **Weston Super Mare** and accessed via the village of **Kewstoke**. Sand Point is an outcrop of Carboniferous Limestone and is very much a smaller version of **Brean Down**. It has very easy footpath access up onto to a wonderful area of plant rich limestone grassland with plants such as Common Centaury, Yellow-Wort, Wild Thyme and Musk Thistle *Cardus nutans*. On the low cliffs grow White Stonecrop, Ivy Broomrape and also the non native Seaside Daisy *Erigeron glaucus* from the coasts of Oregon and California. On the southern side of Sand Point is an area of saltmarsh with Sea Aster and Sea-lavender. Curlew and Oystercatchers can be often be seen here through the summer and a good variety of waders and duck visit during the winter. Owned by the National Trust.

Uphill

Immediately south of **Weston Super Mare** and accessed from **Uphill village**. Uphill is adjacent to **Walborough** and between them they form a very extensive area of plant-rich limestone grassland. Plants found here include Salad Burnet , Fairy Flax *Linum catharticum*, Kidney Vetch, Small Scabious *Scabiosa columbaria* and Hutchinsia *Hornungia petraea*. Butterflies likely to be seen during the summer include Common Blue, Chalkhill Blue and Brown Argus Owned by North Somerset Council

Walborough

Immediately south of **Weston Super Mare** and accessed from **Uphill village** The limestone grassland flora includes the nationally rare Somerset hair-grass *Koleria vallesiana* and Honewort *Trinia glauca*. Also found here are Common Broomrape *Orobanche minor*, Cowslip *Primula veris*, Green-winged and Early-purple Orchids and Autumn Lady's-tresses *Spiranthes spiralis*. Butterflies include Brown Argus, Grizzled and Dingy Skippers and Grayling. The Walborough grasslands run down to an area of salt marsh that has a number of nationally scarce plants including Sea Barley *Hordeum marinium*, Slender

Hare's-ear *Bubleurum tenuissimum* and Sea Clover. Sea-lavender flowers here in late summer. Good numbers of wildfowl and waders occur here, and on the adjacent River Axe estuary, during autumn and winter, including Redshank, Dunlin, Shelduck and Black-tailed Godwit. Owned by Avon Wildlife Trust

Steep Holm

Steep Holm is not part of the modern county of Somerset, but it is a very obvious coastal feature standing sentinel in the sea, and can be seen from a large proportion of the Somerset coast. Since 1996 Steep Holm has been part of the administrative area of North Somerset. The west coasts of the UK play a key role in helping to maintain Europe's seabird populations. Steep Holm despite not having Puffins or Gannets is, without doubt, an important part of that network of island seabird breeding sites. In particular it plays an important role in maintaining the seabird biodiversity of Somerset's coast and the Severn Estuary. Many of the seagulls that you will see on this coast will have hatched on Steep Holm.

The island has a stunning seabird colony composed mainly of Herring Gulls and Lesser Black- backed Gulls with a small number of Greater Black-backed Gulls, Cormorants and Shelduck.

During May, June and July it is a real wildlife spectacle with the top of the island, the cliffs and the sky, alive with a swirling mass of noisy dive-bombing gulls. The aerial prowess of all these gulls is a wonderful thing to watch as they make expert use of the fierce winds blowing up off the sea, often hanging effortlessly in the sky before a plunging steeply to the sea below.

Herring Gull – The UK has 175,000 breeding pairs. Numbers have been in decline for a considerable time and they are now on the Red List of Birds of Conservation Concern. Somerset currently has about 450 breeding pairs, following a decline of over 75% since the 1970s. Steep Holm has about 1,300 breeding pairs.

Lesser Black-backed Gull – The UK has around 112,000 breeding pairs. Although numbers have fluctuated less than the other gulls they are still on the Amber List of Birds of Conservation Concern due to big declines in some parts of the UK. Somerset is thought to have about 100 breeding pairs. Steep Holm has approximately 450 breeding pairs.

Greater Black-backed Gull – The UK has about 17,000 breeding pairs. Some parts of the UK have seen very big declines in this gull and in consequence

they are on the Amber List of Birds of Conservation Concern. Somerset now has 1–2 breeding pairs following a 90% decline since 1970s. Steep Holm has about 13 breeding pairs.

Cormorant – The UK has about 8,000 pairs of coastal breeding Cormorants. Somerset has 20 breeding pairs inland and none on the coast. Steep Holm has approximately 100 breeding pairs.

Shelduck – Ther are about 10,000 breeding pairs in UK. Somerset has approximately six breeding pairs. Steepholm has 5 breeding pairs.

Steep Holm is owned and managed by the Kenneth Allsop Memorial Trust (www.steepholm.org.uk), Boat trips go to Steep Holm from Knightstone Harbour in Weston Super Mare.

DEVON

Foreland Point

Foreland Point can be reached from the South West Coast Path or by parking mid way between **County Gate** and **Lynton** and then walking down the track that leads to Foreland Point light house. This dramatic zig-zag track passes through some fine heathland habitat. Mid July is the height of the flowering season here and you can see Bell Heather and Cross-leaved Heath, Eyebright *Euphorbia nemerosa*, Lousewort *Pedicularis sylvatica* and Common Dodder among many other plants.

Gannets are likely to be seen out over the sea here throughout the summer, they travel from the Pembrokshire islands where they breed. It is also a very good spot for watching Herring Gulls, Lesser Black- backed Gulls and Greater Black-backed Gulls carrying out aerial acrobatics over the sea. Owned by the National Trust

Lynmouth

Lynton and Lynmouth are well known holiday destinations but the beach at Lynmouth is well worth visiting just for its marine life. The seaweed diversity is high here and the causeway that heads out into the sea on the west side of the harbour gives good, relatively flat, access to seaweed-covered boulders and rock pools as the tide drops. In particular look out for the robust crinkled Sugar Kelp *Saccharina latissima* and the red seaweeds Sea Oak *Phycodrys rubens* and Red Comb Weed *Plocamium cartilagineum*. One of the commonest molluscs found in the rockpools is the Grey Top Shell *Gibbula cineraria*. Exmoor National Park staff often run beach walks to identify shore life during the summer.

Sand Point

Common Broomrape, Walborough

Lesser Black-backed Gull, Steep Holm

Eyebright, Foreland Point

Grey Top Shell, Lynmouth

APPENDIX 2
Conservation status of the Somerset coast

NATURE RESERVES

Berrow Dunes Local Nature Reserve –
Size 17 ha
Managed by Sedgemoor District Council

**Bridgwater Bay National Nature
Reserve** – Size 2,559 ha
Managed by Natural England

**Huntspill River National Nature
Reserve** – Size 148 ha
Managed by the Environment Agency

SITES OF SPECIAL SCIENTIFIC
INTEREST (SSSI) designated by Natural
England

Brean Down SSSI - Size 65.1 ha
Biological SSSI: plant-rich Carboniferous
limestone grassland, rare plants and
insects. Geological SSSI: Devensian
deposits.

Berrow Dunes SSSI – Size 200 ha
Biological SSSI: coastal habitats, sand
dunes and dune slacks, diverse flora, rich
invertebrate fauna.

Bridgwater Bay SSSI – Size 3,574.1 ha
Biological SSSI: intertidal mudflats,
saltmarsh and shingle. Internationally
and nationally important passage
migrant and wintering waders and
wildfowl.

Blue Anchor to Lilstock SSSI –
Size 742.8 ha
Geological SSSI: coastal
geomorphology, wave cut intertidal rock
platforms. Jurassic and Triassic cliffs and
Pleistocene deposits.

Exmoor Coastal Heaths SSSI –
Size 1,758.3 but part in Devon
Biological SSSI: extensive area of coastal
heathland, acidic and maritime
grassland.

**Porlock Shingle Ridge and Saltmarsh
SSSI** – Size 186.29 ha
Biological SSSI: nationally important
saltmarsh and shingle vegetation.
Geological SSSI: large shingle ridge and
active coastal geomorphology.

Glenthorne SSSI – Size 13.3 ha
Geological SSSI: Devonian, Hangman
Sandstone cliffs.

UK AND EUROPEAN DESIGNATIONS

Severn Estuary SAC – Size 73,715.4 ha
A Special Area of Conservation or SAC
is defined in the European Union's

Porlock Shingle Ridge & Saltmarsh SSSI

Exmoor Coastal Heaths SSSI

Blue Anchor to Lilstock SSSI

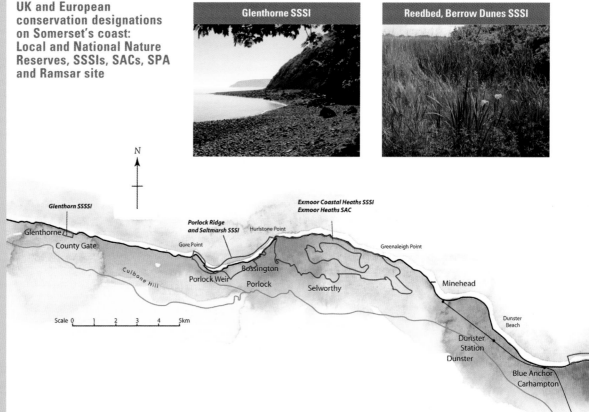

UK and European
conservation designations
on Somerset's coast:
Local and National Nature
Reserves, SSSIs, SACs, SPA
and Ramsar site

Glenthorne SSSI

Reedbed, Berrow Dunes SSSI

Glenthorn SSSSI

Glenthorne

County Gate

*Porlock Ridge
and Saltmarsh SSSI*

Hurlstone Point

Gore Point

*Exmoor Coastal Heaths SSSI
Exmoor Heaths SAC*

Greenaleigh Point

Culbone Hill

Porlock Weir

Bossington

Porlock

Selworthy

Minehead

Scale 0 1 2 3 4 5km

Dunster
Beach

Dunster
Station

Dunster

Blue Anchor
Carhampton

Habitats Directive, also known as the Directive on the Conservation of Natural Habitats and of Wild Fauna and Flora. They are to protect the 220 habitats and approximately 1,000 species listed in Annex I and II of the Directive which are considered to be of European interest following criteria given in the Directive.

Severn Estuary SPA – Size 24,662.98 ha (part of the above SAC)

A Special Protection Area or SPA is a designation under the European Union Directive on the Conservation of Wild Birds. Under this Directive, Member States of the European Union have a duty to safeguard the habitats of migratory birds and certain particularly threatened birds. Together with SACs, the SPAs form a network of protected sites across the European Union, called Natura 2000.

Severn Estuary Ramsar site – Size 24, 662.98 ha (covers the same area as the above SPA)

The Ramsar Convention (The Convention on Wetlands of International Importance, especially as Waterfowl Habitat) is an international treaty for the conservation and sustainable utilisation of wetlands, i.e., to stem the progressive encroachment on and loss of wetlands now and in the future, recognising the fundamental ecological functions of wetlands and their economic, cultural, scientific, and recreational value. It is named after the town of Ramsar in Iran. The convention was developed and adopted by participating nations at a meeting in Ramsar on 2 February 1971, and came into force on 21 December 1975. The Ramsar List of Wetlands of International Importance now includes 1,888 sites covering around 1,853,000 km²

Severn Estuary Marine Protected Area

An overarching description that covers the Severn Estuary SPA and SAC areas. Marine Protected Area (MPA) is a term used to describe "any area of intertidal or subtidal terrain, together with its overlying water and associated flora, fauna, historical and cultural features, which has been reserved by law or other effective means to protect part or all of the enclosed environment". The protection afforded is aimed at reducing destruction, damage or the reduction in distribution of marine species and/or habitats.

In the UK, MPAs are set up primarily for the conservation of our marine biodiversity and to protect species and habitats of international or national importance. The main types of MPA in the UK are SACs. SACs, in addition to Marine Nature Reserves (MNRs) and SPAs, are protected by statutory obligations. The UK also has voluntary MPAs such as Voluntary Marine Conservation Areas (VMCAs) and Voluntary Marine Nature Reserves (VMNRs).

Exmoor Heaths SAC – Size 10,705.87 ha

The Exmoor Heaths SAC covers heathland on the coast cliff tops in Somerset and Devon. It also includes heathland that occurs well inland.

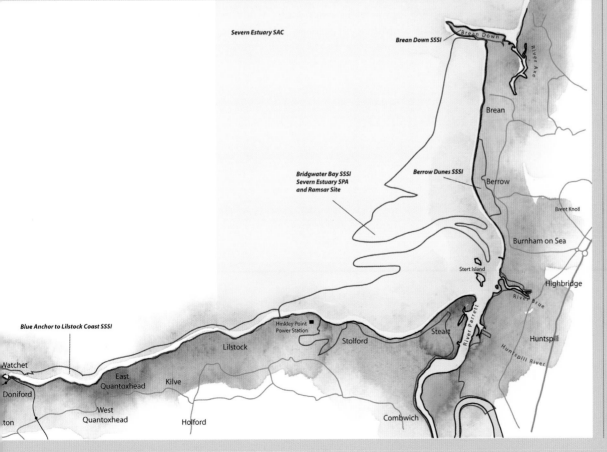

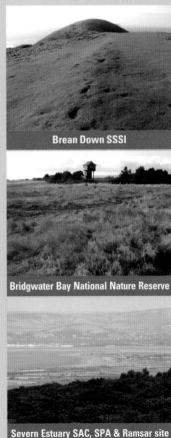

Brean Down SSSI

Bridgwater Bay National Nature Reserve

Severn Estuary SAC, SPA & Ramsar site

APPENDIX 3
Seaweeds

Juliet Brodie[1] and Nigel Chaffey[2]
1 Natural History Museum, Department of Botany, Cromwell Road, London SW7 5BD, UK
2 Bath Spa University, Department of Science, Newton St. Loe, Bath BA2 9BN, UK

Species list based on collections made between 2008 and 2010 at the following sites: Portishead, Clevedon, Anchor Head (Weston-super-Mare), Sand Bay, Brean Down, Lilstock, Kilve, Blue Anchor Bay, Hurlstone Point and Porlock.

Pepper Dulse

Dulse

Red Comb Weed

Gut Weed

RHODOPHYTA – red algae
Acrochaetium secundatum
Aglaothamnion hookeri
Bangia fuscopurpurea
 Velvet Thread Weed
Bostrychia scorpioides
 Scorpion-tailed Saltmarsh Weed
Calliblepharis ciliata
 Beautiful Eyelash Weed
Callithamnion tetricum
Catenella caespitosa
 Creeping Chain Weed
Ceramium botryocarpum
Ceramium ciliatum
Ceramium deslongchampii
Ceramium pallidum
Ceramium secundatum
Ceramium virgatum
Chondracanthus acicularis **Creephorn**
Chondrus crispus **Irish Moss**
Corallina caespitosa **Tufted Coral Weed**
Corallina officinalis
 Common Coral Weed
Cryptopleua ramosa
 Fine-leaved Crinkle Weed
Cystoclonium purpureum
 Purple Claw Weed
Dilsea carnea
Dumontia contorta
 Dumont's Tubular Weed
Erythrocladia irregularis
Furcellaria fastigiata
Gelidium pusillum
Gracilaria gracilis **Slender Wart Weed**
Heterosiphonia plumosa
 Siphoned Feather Weed

Hildenbrandia crouanii
Hildenbrandia rubra
Holmsiella pachyderma
Hypoglossum hypoglossoides
 Under Tongue Weed
Laurencia hybrida
Lithophyllum incrustans
 Common Pale Paint Weed
Lomentaria articulata
 Bunny-eared Bead Weed
Mastocarpus stellatus **Grape Pip Weed**
Membranoptera alata **Winged Weed**
Osmundea osmunda **Royal Fern Weed**
Osmundea pinnatifida **Pepper Dulse**
Osmundea ramosissima
 Branched Fern Weed
Palmaria palmata **Dulse**
Petrocelis cruenta
Phymatolithon lenormandii
 Common Shore Paint Weed
Plocamium cartilagineum
 Red Comb Weed
Polyides rotundus **Discoid Fork Weed**
Polysiphonia fucoides **Black Siphon Weed**
Polysiphonia lanosa **Wrack Siphon Weed**
Polysiphonia stricta **Pitcher Siphon Weed**
Porphyra purpurea **Purple Laver**
Porphyra umbilicalis **Tough Laver**
Rhodochorton purpureum
Rhodothamniella floridula **Sand Binder**
Sahlingia subintegra

CHLOROPHYTA – green algae
Blidingia marginata
Blidingia minima
Chaetomorpha melagonium

Cladophora cf. sericea
Cladophora laetevirens
Cladophora lehmanniana
Cladophora rupestris
 Common Green Branched Weed
Cladophora vagabunda
Derbesia tenuissima **Silky Thread Weed**
Prasiola stipitata
Rhizoclonium riparium
 Rooting Green Thread Weed
Syncoryne reinkei
Ulva compressa **Thead Weed**
Ulva intestinalis **Gut Weed**
Ulva lactuca **Sea Lettuce**
Ulva linza **Doubled Ribbon Weed**
Ulva prolifera
Ulva pseudocurvata
Urospora penicilliformis

PHAEOPHYCEAE – brown algae
Ascophyllum nodosum **Egg Wrack**
Cladostephus spongiosus
 Hairy Sand Weed
Dictyota dichotoma **Divided Net Weed**
Ectocarpus confervoides
Ectocarpus siliculosus
Elachista fucicola **Tiny Wrack Bush**
Fucus serratus **Toothed Wrack**
Fucus spiralis **Spiral Wrack**
Fucus vesiculosus **Bladder Wrack**
Laminaria digitata **Oar Weed**
Laminaria hyperborea **Forest Kelp**
Pelvetia canaliculata **Channelled Wrack**
Pilayella littoralis
Ralfsia verrucosa
Spongonema tomentosum **Lamb's Tails**

APPENDIX 4
Plants

This list does not claim to include every plant found along the coast. It does however give an indication of the great plant diversity that can be found. This is principally due to the landscape diversity along the coast brought about by having Exmoor, the Quantocks, the Mendips and the Somerset Levels as the backdrop to it. It also includes a fair number of garden escapes that occur regularly, particularly on the dune areas.

Taxus baccata **Yew**
Nymphaea alba **White Water-lily**
Ceratophyllum demersum
Rigid Hornwort
Ceratophyllum submersum
Soft Hornwort
Caltha palustris **Marsh-marigold**
Helleborus foetidus **Stinking Hellebore**
Anemone nemorosa **Wood Anemone**
Clematis vitalba **Traveller's-joy**
Ranunculus acris **Meadow Buttercup**
Ranunculus aquatilis
Common Water-crowfoot
Ranunculus auricomus
Goldilocks Buttercup
Ranunculus bulbosus
Bulbous Buttercup
Ranunculus ficaria **Lesser Celandine**
Ranunculus flammula
Lesser Spearwort
Ranunculus parviflorus
Small-flowered Buttercup
Ranunculus repens **Creeping Buttercup**
Ranunculus sardous **Hairy Buttercup**
Ranunculus sceleratus
Celery-leaved Buttercup
Ranunculus baudotii
Brackish Water-crowfoot
Ranunculus hederaceus
Ivy-leaved Crowfoot
Ranunculus omiophyllus
Round-leaved Crowfoot
Ranunculus penicillatus
Stream Water-crowfoot
Ranunculus trichophyllus
Thread-leaved Water-crowfoot
Aquilegia vulgaris **Columbine**
Thalictrum flavum
Common Meadow-rue
Thalictrum minus **Lesser Meadow-rue**
Papaver argemone **Prickly Poppy**
Papaver atlanticum **Atlas Poppy**
Papaver dubium **Long-headed Poppy**
Papaver pseudoorientale
Oriental Poppy
Papaver rhoeas **Common Poppy**
Papaver somniferum **Opium Poppy**
Meconopsis cambrica **Welsh Poppy**
Glaucium flavum **Yellow Horned-poppy**
Chelidonium majus **Greater Celandine**
Pseudofumaria lutea **Yellow Corydalis**
Fumaria bastardii **Tall Ramping-fumitory**

Fumaria capreolata
White Ramping-fumitory
Fumaria muralis
Common Ramping-fumitory
Fumaria officinalis **Common Fumitory**
Ulmus glabra **Wych Elm**
Ulmus procera **English Elm**
Humulus lupulus **Hop**
Urtica dioica **Common Nettle**
Urtica urens **Small Nettle**
Parietaria judaica **Pellitory-of-the-wall**
Fagus sylvatica **Beech**
Castanea sativa **Sweet Chestnut**
Quercus cerris **Turkey Oak**
Quercus ilex **Evergreen Oak**
Quercus petraea **Sessile Oak**
Quercus robur **Pedunculate Oak**
Betula pendula **Silver Birch**
Betula pubescens **Downy Birch**
Alnus glutinosa **Alder**
Corylus avellana **Hazel**
Carpinus betulus **Hornbeam**
Chenopodium album **Fat-hen**
Chenopodium ficifolium
Fig-leaved Goosefoot
Chenopodium murale
Nettle-leaved Goosefoot
Chenopodium polyspermum
Many-seeded Goosefoot
Chenopodium rubrum **Red Goosefoot**
Atriplex glabriuscula
Babington's Orache
Atriplex halimus **Shrubby Orache**
Atriplex laciniata **Frosted Orache**
Atriplex littoralis **Grass-leaved Orache**
Atriplex longipes **Long-stalked Orache**
Atriplex patula **Common Orache**
Atriplex portulacoides **Sea-purslane**
Atriplex prostrata **Spear-leaved Orache**
Beta vulgaris ssp. *maritima* **Sea Beet**
Salicornia dolichostachya
Long-spiked Glasswort
Salicornia europaea
Common Glasswort
Salicornia fragilis **Yellow Glasswort**
Salicornia pusilla
One-flowered Glasswort
Salicornia ramosissima
Purple Glasswort
Suaeda maritima **Annual Sea-blite**
Salsola kali ssp. *kali* **Prickly Saltwort**
Montia fontana **Blinks**

Claytonia perfoliata **Springbeauty**
Arenaria serpyllifolia
Thyme-leaved Sandwort
Arenaria serpyllifolia ssp. *leptoclados*
Slender Sandwort
Moehringia trinervia
Three-nerved Sandwort
Honckenya peploides **Sea Sandwort**
Stellaria uliginosa **Bog Stitchwort**
Stellaria graminea **Lesser Stitchwort**
Stellaria holostea **Greater Stitchwort**
Stellaria media **Common Chickweed**
Stellaria neglecta **Greater Chickweed**
Stellaria pallida **Lesser Chickweed**
Cerastium arvense **Field Mouse-ear**
Cerastium diffusum **Sea Mouse-ear**
Cerastium fontanum
Common Mouse-ear
Cerastium glomeratum
Sticky Mouse-ear
Cerastium pumilum **Dwarf Mouse-ear**
Cerastium semidecandrum
Little Mouse-ear
Cerastium tomentosum
Snow-in-summer
Moenchia erecta **Upright Chickweed**
Myosoton aquaticum
Water Chickweed
Sagina apetala **Annual Pearlwort**
Sagina maritima **Sea Pearlwort**
Sagina procumbens
Procumbent Pearlwort
Spergula arvensis **Corn Spurrey**
Spergularia marina **Lesser Sea-spurrey**
Spergularia media **Greater Sea-spurrey**
Spergularia rubra **Sand Spurrey**
Spergularia rupicola **Rock Sea-spurrey**
Lychnis flos-cuculi **Ragged-Robin**
Silene conica **Sand Catchfly**
Silene dioica **Red Campion**
Silene latifolia **White Campion**
Silene uniflora **Sea Campion**
Silene vulgaris **Bladder Campion**
Saponaria officinalis **Soapwort**
Persicaria amphibia
Amphibious Bistort
Persicaria bistorta **Common Bistort**
Persicaria hydropiper **Water-pepper**
Persicaria lapathifolia **Pale Persicaria**
Persicaria maculosa **Redshank**
Persicaria wallichii
Himalayan Knotweed

White Ramping-fumitory

Annual Sea-blight

Sea Sandwort

Rock Sea-spurrey

Red Campion

Polygonum arenastrum
Equal-leaved Knotgrass
Polygonum aviculare **Knotgrass**
Polygonum oxyspermum
Ray's Knotgrass
Fallopia baldschuanica **Russian-vine**
Fallopia convolvulus **Black-bindweed**
Fallopia japonica **Japanese Knotweed**
Fallopia sachalinensis **Giant Knotweed**
Rumex acetosa **Common Sorrel**
Rumex acetosella **Sheep's Sorrel**
Rumex conglomeratus **Clustered Dock**
Rumex crispus **Curled Dock**
Rumex cristatus **Greek Dock**
Rumex hydrolapathum **Water Dock**
Rumex maritimus **Golden Dock**
Rumex obtusifolius **Broad-leaved Dock**
Rumex palustris **Marsh Dock**
Rumex pulcher **Fiddle Dock**
Limonium binervosum
Rock Sea-lavender
Limonium vulgare
Common Sea-lavender
Armeria maritima **Thrift**
Hypericum androsaemum **Tutsan**
Hypericum calycinum **Rose-of-Sharon**
Hypericum hirsutum
Hairy St John's-wort
Hypericum humifusum
Trailing St John's-wort
Hypericum montanum
Pale St John's-wort
Hypericum perforatum
Perforate St John's-wort
Hypericum pulchrum
Slender St John's-wort
Hypericum tetrapterum
Square-stalked St John's-wort
Tilia platyphyllos **Large-leaved Lime**
Tilia platyphyllos x *cordata* =
T. x *europaea* **Lime**
Malva moschata **Musk-mallow**
Malva neglecta **Dwarf Mallow**
Malva sylvestris **Common Mallow**
Lavatera arborea **Tree-mallow**
Althaea officinalis **Marsh-mallow**
Alcea rosea **Hollyhock**
Helianthemum apenninum
White Rock-rose
Helianthemum nummularium
Common Rock-rose
Viola arvensis **Field Pansy**
Viola canina **Heath Dog-violet**
Viola hirta **Hairy Violet**
Viola odorata **Sweet Violet**
Viola reichenbachiana **Early Dog-violet**
Viola riviniana **Common Dog-violet**
Tamarix gallica **Tamarisk**
Bryonia dioica **White Bryony**
Populus alba **White Poplar**
Populus nigra **Black-poplar**
Populus tremula **Aspen**
Salix alba **White Willow**
Salix aurita **Eared Willow**

Salix caprea **Goat Willow**
Salix cinerea ssp. *oleifolia* **Rusty Willow**
Salix fragilis **Crack-willow**
Salix purpurea **Purple Willow**
Salix repens **Creeping Willow**
Salix triandra **Almond Willow**
Salix viminalis **Osier**
Sisymbrium officinale **Hedge Mustard**
Sisymbrium orientale **Eastern Rocket**
Alliaria petiolata **Garlic Mustard**
Arabidopsis thaliana **Thale Cress**
Erysimum cheiri **Wallflower**
Matthiola incana **Hoary Stock**
Barbarea vulgaris **Winter-cress**
Rorippa nasturtium-aquaticum
Water-cress
Armoracia rusticana **Horse-radish**
Cardamine flexuosa **Wavy Bitter-cress**
Cardamine hirsuta **Hairy Bitter-cress**
Cardamine pratensis **Cuckooflower**
Erophila verna **Common Whitlowgrass**
Cochlearia anglica **English Scurvygrass**
Cochlearia danica **Danish Scurvygrass**
Cochlearia officinalis
Common Scurvygrass
Capsella bursa-pastoris
Shepherd's-purse
Thlaspi arvense **Field Penny-cress**
Lepidium campestre **Field Pepperwort**
Lepidium draba **Hoary Cress**
Lepidium heterophyllum
Smith's Pepperwort
Coronopus didymus **Lesser Swine-cress**
Coronopus squamatus **Swine-cress**
Diplotaxis muralis **Annual Wall-rocket**
Brassica napus **Rape**
Brassica napus ssp. *oleifera*
Oil-seed Rape
Brassica nigra **Black Mustard**
Brassica rapa ssp. *campestris*
Wild Turnip
Sinapis arvensis **Charlock**
Cakile maritima **Sea Rocket**
Hirschfeldia incana **Hoary Mustard**
Raphanus raphanistrum ssp. *maritimus*
Sea Radish
Raphanus raphanistrum ssp. *raphanistrum*
Wild Radish
Reseda lutea **Wild Mignonette**
Reseda luteola **Weld**
Rhododendron ponticum **Rhododendron**
Calluna vulgaris **Heather**
Erica cinerea **Bell Heather**
Erica tetralix **Cross-leaved Heath**
Vaccinium myrtillus **Bilberry**
Primula veris **Cowslip**
Primula vulgaris **Primrose**
Primula vulgaris x *veris* = *P.* x *polyantha*
False Oxlip
Lysimachia nemorum **Yellow Pimpernel**
Lysimachia nummularia **Creeping-Jenny**
Lysimachia vulgaris **Yellow Loosestrife**
Anagallis arvensis **Scarlet Pimpernel**
Glaux maritima **Sea-milkwort**

Samolus valerandi **Brookweed**
Ribes nigrum **Black Currant**
Ribes rubrum **Red Currant**
Ribes sanguineum **Flowering Currant**
Crassula helmsii
New Zealand Pigmyweed
Crassula tillaea **Mossy Stonecrop**
Umbilicus rupestris **Navelwort**
Sedum acre **Biting Stonecrop**
Sedum album **White Stonecrop**
Sedum anglicum **English Stonecrop**
Sedum forsterianum **Rock Stonecrop**
Sedum rupestre **Reflexed Stonecrop**
Saxifraga tridactylites
Rue-leaved Saxifrage
Chrysosplenium oppositifolium
Opposite-leaved Golden-saxifrage
Filipendula ulmaria **Meadowsweet**
Filipendula vulgaris **Dropwort**
Rubus caesius **Dewberry**
Rubus fruticosus **Bramble**
Rubus idaeus **Raspberry**
Potentilla anglica **Trailing Tormentil**
Potentilla anserina **Silverweed**
Potentilla erecta **Tormentil**
Potentilla reptans **Creeping Cinquefoil**
Potentilla sterilis **Barren Strawberry**
Fragaria vesca **Wild Strawberry**
Geum urbanum **Wood Avens**
Agrimonia eupatoria **Agrimony**
Sanguisorba minor **Salad Burnet**
Alchemilla filicaulis ssp. *vestita*
Southern Lady's-mantle
Alchemilla mollis **Garden Lady's-mantle**
Alchemilla xanthochlora
Pale Lady's-mantle
Aphanes arvensis **Parsley-piert**
Aphanes australis
Slender Parsley-piert
Rosa agrestis **Small-leaved Sweet-briar**
Rosa arvensis **Field-rose**
Rosa canina **Dog-rose**
Rosa rubiginosa **Sweet-briar**
Rosa sherardii **Sherard's Downy-rose**
Rosa spinosissima **Burnet Rose**
Rosa stylosa **Short-styled Field-rose**
Prunus avium **Wild Cherry**
Prunus cerasifera **Cherry Plum**
Prunus domestica **Wild Plum**
Prunus laurocerasus **Cherry Laurel**
Prunus spinosa **Blackthorn**
Malus sylvestris **Crab Apple**
Malus domestica **Apple**
Sorbus aucuparia **Rowan**
Sorbus aria **Common Whitebeam**
Sorbus subcuneata
Somerset Whitebeam
Sorbus vexans **Bloody Whitebeam**
Cotoneaster horizontalis
Wall Cotoneaster
Crataegus monogyna **Hawthorn**
Anthyllis vulneraria **Kidney Vetch**
Lotus corniculatus
Common Bird's-foot-trefoil

Rock Stonecrop

Kidney Vetch

Alexanders

Bugloss

Wild Marjoram

Lotus pedunculatus
Greater Bird's-foot-trefoil
Lotus subbiflorus
Hairy Bird's-foot-trefoil
Ornithopus perpusillus **Bird's-foot**
Hippocrepis comosa **Horseshoe Vetch**
Vicia bithynica **Bithynian Vetch**
Vicia cracca **Tufted Vetch**
Vicia hirsuta **Hairy Tare**
Vicia lathyroides **Spring Vetch**
Vicia parviflora **Slender Tare**
Vicia sativa **Common Vetch**
Vicia sepium **Bush Vetch**
Vicia sylvatica **Wood Vetch**
Vicia tetrasperma **Smooth Tare**
Lathyrus latifolius
Broad-leaved Everlasting-pea
Lathyrus sylvestris
Narrow-leaved Everlasting-pea
Lathyrus linifolius **Bitter-vetch**
Lathyrus nissolia **Grass Vetchling**
Lathyrus pratensis **Meadow Vetchling**
Onobrychis viciifolia **Sainfoin**
Ononis repens **Common Restharrow**
Ononis spinosa **Spiny Restharrow**
Melilotus albus **White Melilot**
Melilotus altissimus **Tall Melilot**
Melilotus officinalis **Ribbed Melilot**
Medicago arabica **Spotted Medick**
Medicago lupulina **Black Medick**
Medicago polymorpha **Toothed Medick**
Medicago sativa **Lucerne**
Trifolium arvense **Hare's-foot Clover**
Trifolium campestre **Hop Trefoil**
Trifolium dubium **Lesser Trefoil**
Trifolium fragiferum **Strawberry Clover**
Trifolium glomeratum **Clustered Clover**
Trifolium hybridum **Alsike Clover**
Trifolium medium **Zigzag Clover**
Trifolium micranthum **Slender Trefoil**
Trifolium ornithopodioides
Bird's-foot Clover
Trifolium pratense **Red Clover**
Trifolium repens **White Clover**
Trifolium scabrum **Rough Clover**
Trifolium squamosum **Sea Clover**
Trifolium striatum **Knotted Clover**
Trifolium subterraneum
Subterranean Clover
Trifolium suffocatum **Suffocated Clover**
Cytisus scoparius **Broom**
Genista tinctoria **Dyer's Greenweed**
Ulex europaeus **Gorse**
Ulex gallii **Western Gorse**
Hippophae rhamnoides **Sea-buckthorn**
Myriophyllum spicatum
Spiked Water-milfoil
Lythrum salicaria **Purple-loosestrife**
Daphne laureola **Spurge-laurel**
Epilobium ciliatum
American Willowherb
Epilobium hirsutum **Great Willowherb**
Epilobium lanceolatum
Spear-leaved Willowherb

Epilobium montanum
Broad-leaved Willowherb
Epilobium obscurum
Short-fruited Willowherb
Epilobium palustre **Marsh Willowherb**
Epilobium parviflorum
Hoary Willowherb
Epilobium tetragonum
Square-stalked Willowherb
Chamerion angustifolium
Rosebay Willowherb
Oenothera biennis
Common Evening-primrose
Oenothera cambrica
Small-flowered Evening-primrose
Oenothera glazioviana
Large-flowered Evening-primrose
Oenothera stricta
Fragrant Evening-primrose
Circaea lutetiana
Enchanter's-nightshade
Cornus sanguinea **Dogwood**
Viscum album **Mistletoe**
Euonymus europaeus **Spindle**
Ilex aquifolium **Holly**
Mercurialis annua **Annual Mercury**
Mercurialis perennis **Dog's Mercury**
Euphorbia amygdaloides **Wood Spurge**
Euphorbia exigua **Dwarf Spurge**
Euphorbia helioscopia **Sun Spurge**
Euphorbia lathyris **Caper Spurge**
Euphorbia paralias **Sea Spurge**
Euphorbia peplus **Petty Spurge**
Euphorbia platyphyllos
Broad-leaved Spurge
Rhamnus cathartica **Buckthorn**
Linum bienne **Pale Flax**
Linum catharticum **Fairy Flax**
Linum usitatissimum **Flax**
Polygala serpyllifolia **Heath Milkwort**
Polygala vulgaris **Common Milkwort**
Acer campestre **Field Maple**
Acer platanoides **Norway Maple**
Acer pseudoplatanus **Sycamore**
Oxalis acetosella **Wood-sorrel**
Oxalis articulata **Pink-sorrel**
Oxalis corniculata
Procumbent Yellow-sorrel
Oxalis incarnata **Pale Pink-sorrel**
Oxalis latifolia **Garden Pink-sorrel**
Oxalis stricta **Upright Yellow-sorrel**
Geranium columbinum
Long-stalked Crane's-bill
Geranium dissectum
Cut-leaved Crane's-bill
Geranium lucidum **Shining Crane's-bill**
Geranium molle **Dove's-foot Crane's-bill**
Geranium pratense **Meadow Crane's-bill**
Geranium pusillum
Small-flowered Crane's-bill
Geranium pyrenaicum
Hedgerow Crane's-bill
Geranium robertianum **Herb-Robert**
Erodium cicutarium **Common Stork's-bill**

Erodium maritimum **Sea Stork's-bill**
Erodium moschatum **Musk Stork's-bill**
Impatiens glandulifera **Indian Balsam**
Hedera helix **Ivy**
Hedera hibernica **Atlantic Ivy**
Hydrocotyle vulgaris **Marsh Pennywort**
Sanicula europaea **Sanicle**
Chaerophyllum temulum **Rough Chervil**
Anthriscus caucalis **Bur Chervil**
Anthriscus sylvestris **Cow Parsley**
Smyrnium olusatrum **Alexanders**
Conopodium majus **Pignut**
Pimpinella saxifraga **Burnet-saxifrage**
Aegopodium podagraria **Ground-elder**
Berula erecta **Lesser Water-parsnip**
Crithmum maritimum **Rock Samphire**
Oenanthe aquatica
Fine-leaved Water-dropwort
Oenanthe crocata
Hemlock Water-dropwort
Oenanthe fistulosa
Tubular Water-dropwort
Oenanthe lachenalii
Parsley Water-dropwort
Oenanthe pimpinelloides
Corky-fruited Water-dropwort
Aethusa cynapium **Fool's Parsley**
Foeniculum vulgare **Fennel**
Aethusa cynapium ssp. *cynapium*
Fool's Parsley
Silaum silaus **Pepper-saxifrage**
Conium maculatum **Hemlock**
Bupleurum tenuissimum
Slender Hare's-ear
Apium graveolens **Wild Celery**
Apium nodiflorum **Fool's-water-cress**
Petroselinum segetum **Corn Parsley**
Sison amomum **Stone Parsley**
Angelica sylvestris **Wild Angelica**
Pastinaca sativa **Wild Parsnip**
Heracleum mantegazzianum
Giant Hogweed
Heracleum sphondylium **Hogweed**
Torilis arvensis
Spreading Hedge-parsley
Torilis japonica **Upright Hedge-parsley**
Torilis nodosa **Knotted Hedge-parsley**
Daucus carota **Wild Carrot**
Centaurium erythraea
Common Centaury
Centaurium pulchellum **Lesser Centaury**
Blackstonia perfoliata **Yellow-wort**
Gentianella amarella **Autumn Gentian**
Vinca major **Greater Periwinkle**
Vinca minor **Lesser Periwinkle**
Hyoscyamus niger **Henbane**
Lycium barbarum
Duke of Argyll's Teaplant
Solanum dulcamara **Bittersweet**
Solanum nigrum **Black Nightshade**
Convolvulus arvensis **Field Bindweed**
Calystegia sepium **Hedge Bindweed**
Calystegia silvatica **Large Bindweed**
Calystegia soldanella **Sea Bindweed**

Cuscuta epithymum **Dodder**
Echium vulgare **Viper's-bugloss**
Symphytum officinale **Common Comfrey**
Symphytum orientale **White Comfrey**
Anchusa arvensis **Bugloss**
Pentaglottis sempervirens
Green Alkanet
Myosotis arvensis **Field Forget-me-not**
Myosotis discolor
Changing Forget-me-not
Myosotis laxa **Tufted Forget-me-not**
Myosotis ramosissima
Early Forget-me-not
Myosotis scorpioides
Water Forget-me-not
Myosotis secunda
Creeping Forget-me-not
Cynoglossum officinale **Hound's-tongue**
Verbena officinalis **Vervain**
Stachys arvensis **Field Woundwort**
Stachys officinalis **Betony**
Stachys palustris **Marsh Woundwort**
Stachys sylvatica **Hedge Woundwort**
Ballota nigra **Black Horehound**
Lamiastrum galeobdolon
Yellow Archangel
Lamium album **White Dead-nettle**
Lamium hybridum
Cut-leaved Dead-nettle
Lamium purpureum **Red Dead-nettle**
Galeopsis tetrahit **Common Hemp-nettle**
Marrubium vulgare **White Horehound**
Scutellaria galericulata **Skullcap**
Teucrium scorodonia **Wood Sage**
Ajuga reptans **Bugle**
Glechoma hederacea **Ground-ivy**
Prunella vulgaris **Selfheal**
Melissa officinalis **Balm**
Clinopodium ascendens
Common Calamint
Clinopodium vulgare **Wild Basil**
Origanum vulgare **Wild Marjoram**
Thymus polytrichus **Wild Thyme**
Lycopus europaeus **Gypsywort**
Mentha aquatica **Water Mint**
Mentha arvensis **Corn Mint**
Mentha spicata **Spear Mint**
Mentha suaveolens **Round-leaved Mint**
Salvia verbenaca **Wild Clary**
Callitriche obtusangula
Blunt-fruited Water-starwort
Callitriche stagnalis
Common Water-starwort
Plantago coronopus
Buck's-horn Plantain
Plantago lanceolata **Ribwort Plantain**
Plantago major **Greater Plantain**
Plantago maritima **Sea Plantain**
Plantago media **Hoary Plantain**
Buddleja davidii **Butterfly-bush**
Fraxinus excelsior **Ash**
Ligustrum vulgare **Wild Privet**
Verbascum lychnitis **White Mullein**
Verbascum thapsus **Great Mullein**

Scrophularia auriculata **Water Figwort**
Scrophularia nodosa **Common Figwort**
Mimulus guttatus **Monkeyflower**
Antirrhinum majus **Snapdragon**
Cymbalaria muralis
  Ivy-leaved Toadflax
Kickxia elatine **Sharp-leaved Fluellen**
Kickxia spuria **Round-leaved Fluellen**
Linaria purpurea **Purple Toadflax**
Linaria vulgaris **Common Toadflax**
Digitalis purpurea **Foxglove**
Erinus alpinus **Fairy Foxglove**
Veronica agrestis
  Green Field-speedwell
Veronica anagallis-aquatica
  Blue Water-speedwell
Veronica arvensis **Wall Speedwell**
Veronica beccabunga **Brooklime**
Veronica catenata
  Pink Water-speedwell
Veronica chamaedrys
  Germander Speedwell
Veronica filiformis **Slender Speedwell**
Veronica hederifolia
  Ivy-leaved Speedwell
Veronica montana **Wood Speedwell**
Veronica officinalis **Heath Speedwell**
Veronica persica
  Common Field-speedwell
Veronica polita **Grey Field-speedwell**
Veronica serpyllifolia
  Thyme-leaved Speedwell
Sibthorpia europaea
  Cornish Moneywort
Melampyrum pratense
  Common Cow-wheat
Euphrasia nemorosa
  Common Eyebright
Odontites vernus **Red Bartsia**
Rhinanthus minor **Yellow-rattle**
Pedicularis sylvatica **Lousewort**
Orobanche hederae **Ivy Broomrape**
Orobanche minor **Common Broomrape**
Campanula portenschlagiana
  Adria Bellflower
Campanula poscharskyana
  Trailing Bellflower
Campanula rotundifolia **Harebell**
Wahlenbergia hederacea
  Ivy-leaved Bellflower
Jasione montana **Sheep's-bit**
Sherardia arvensis **Field Madder**
Galium aparine **Cleavers**
Galium mollugo **Hedge Bedstraw**
Galium odoratum **Woodruff**
Galium palustre **Marsh-bedstraw**
Galium palustre ssp. *elongatum*
  Great Marsh-bedstraw
Galium saxatile **Heath Bedstraw**
Galium uliginosum **Fen Bedstraw**
Galium verum **Lady's Bedstraw**
Cruciata laevipes **Crosswort**
Rubia peregrina **Wild Madder**
Sambucus nigra **Elder**

Viburnum lantana **Wayfaring-tree**
Viburnum opulus **Guelder-rose**
Lonicera periclymenum **Honeysuckle**
Adoxa moschatellina **Moschatel**
Valerianella carinata
  Keeled-fruited Cornsalad
Valerianella locusta **Common Cornsalad**
Valeriana officinalis **Common Valerian**
Centranthus ruber **Red Valerian**
Dipsacus fullonum **Wild Teasel**
Dipsacus pilosus **Small Teasel**
Knautia arvensis **Field Scabious**
Succisa pratensis **Devil's-bit Scabious**
Scabiosa columbaria **Small Scabious**
Arctium lappa **Greater Burdock**
Arctium minus **Lesser Burdock**
Carduus crispus **Welted Thistle**
Carduus nutans **Musk Thistle**
Carduus tenuiflorus **Slender Thistle**
Cirsium acaule **Dwarf Thistle**
Cirsium arvense **Creeping Thistle**
Cirsium eriophorum **Woolly Thistle**
Cirsium palustre **Marsh Thistle**
Cirsium vulgare **Spear Thistle**
Onopordum acanthium **Cotton Thistle**
Silybum marianum **Milk Thistle**
Centaurea montana
  Perennial Cornflower
Centaurea nigra **Common Knapweed**
Centaurea scabiosa **Greater Knapweed**
Cichorium intybus **Chicory**
Lapsana communis **Nipplewort**
Hypochaeris glabra **Smooth Cat's-ear**
Hypochaeris radicata **Cat's-ear**
Leontodon autumnalis **Autumn Hawkbit**
Leontodon hispidus **Rough Hawkbit**
Leontodon saxatilis **Lesser Hawkbit**
Picris echioides **Bristly Oxtongue**
Picris hieracioides
  Hawkweed Oxtongue
Tragopogon pratensis **Goat's-beard**
Sonchus arvensis
  Perennial Sow-thistle
Sonchus asper **Prickly Sow-thistle**
Sonchus oleraceus
  Smooth Sow-thistle
Lactuca serriola **Prickly Lettuce**
Mycelis muralis **Wall Lettuce**
Taraxacum officinalis
  Common Dandelion
Taraxacum oxoniense
  Oxford Dandelion
Taraxacum rubicundum
  Ruddy Dandelion
Crepis capillaris **Smooth Hawk's-beard**
Crepis vesicaria **Beaked Hawk's-beard**
Pilosella aurantiaca **Fox-and-cubs**
Pilosella officinarum
  Mouse-ear-hawkweed
Hieracium acuminatum **Tall Hawkweed**
Hieracium eustomon
  Bristol Channel Hawkweed
Hieracium maculatum
  Spotted Hawkweed

Hieracium sabaudum
  Autumn Hawkweed
Hieracium umbellatum
  Umbellate Hawkweed
Filago vulgaris **Common Cudweed**
Gnaphalium uliginosum
  Marsh Cudweed
Inula conyzae **Ploughman's-spikenard**
Pulicaria dysenterica
  Common Fleabane
Solidago virgaurea **Goldenrod**
Aster lanceolatus
  Narrow-leaved Michaelmas-daisy
Aster linosyris **Goldilocks Aster**
Aster tripolium **Sea Aster**
Erigeron acer **Blue Fleabane**
Erigeron glaucus **Seaside Daisy**
Bellis perennis **Daisy**
Tanacetum parthenium **Feverfew**
Tanacetum vulgare **Tansy**
Seriphidium maritimum
  Sea Wormwood
Carlina vulgaris **Carline Thistle**
Artemisia absinthium **Wormwood**
Artemisia stelleriana **Hoary Mugwort**
Artemisia vulgaris **Mugwort**
Achillea millefolium **Yarrow**
Chamaemelum nobile **Chamomile**
Anthemis cotula **Stinking Chamomile**
Leucanthemum vulgare **Oxeye Daisy**
Matricaria discoidea **Pineappleweed**
Matricaria recutita **Scented Mayweed**
Tripleurospermum inodorum
  Scentless Mayweed
Tripleurospermum maritimum
  Sea Mayweed
Senecio aquaticus **Marsh Ragwort**
Senecio cineraria **Silver Ragwort**
Senecio erucifolius **Hoary Ragwort**
Senecio jacobaea **Common Ragwort**
Senecio squalidus **Oxford Ragwort**
Senecio sylvaticus **Heath Groundsel**
Senecio viscosus **Sticky Groundsel**
Senecio vulgaris **Groundsel**
Tussilago farfara **Coltsfoot**
Petasites hybridus **Butterbur**
Petasites fragrans **Winter Heliotrope**
Bidens tripartita **Trifid Bur-marigold**
Eupatorium cannabinum
  Hemp-agrimony
Butomus umbellatus **Flowering-rush**
Alisma plantago-aquatica
  Water-plantain
Hydrocharis morsus-ranae **Frogbit**
Elodea canadensis
  Canadian Waterweed
Elodea nuttallii **Nuttall's Waterweed**
Triglochin maritimum **Sea Arrowgrass**
Triglochin palustre **Marsh Arrowgrass**
Potamogeton berchtoldii
  Small Pondweed
Potamogeton crispus **Curled Pondweed**
Potamogeton lucens
  Shining Pondweed

Sheep's-bit

Wild Madder

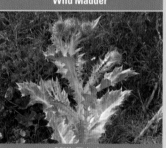
Milk Thistle

Three-cornered Leek

Heath Spotted-orchid

Potamogeton natans
Broad-leaved Pondweed
Potamogeton pectinatus
Fennel Pondweed
Potamogeton pusillus
Lesser Pondweed
Ruppia maritima **Beaked Tasselweed**
Zannichellia palustris
Horned Pondweed
Arum italicum **Italian Lords-and-Ladies**
Arum maculatum **Lords-and-Ladies**
Spirodela polyrhiza **Greater Duckweed**
Lemna gibba **Fat Duckweed**
Lemna minor **Common Duckweed**
Lemna minuta **Least Duckweed**
Lemna trisulca **Ivy-leaved Duckweed**
Wolffia arrhiza **Rootless Duckweed**
Juncus acutiflorus
Sharp-flowered Rush
Juncus acutus **Sharp Rush**
Juncus ambiguus **Frog Rush**
Juncus articulatus **Jointed Rush**
Juncus bufonius **Toad Rush**
Juncus bulbosus **Bulbous Rush**
Juncus conglomeratus **Compact Rush**
Juncus effusus **Soft-rush**
Juncus gerardii **Saltmarsh Rush**
Juncus inflexus **Hard Rush**
Juncus maritimus **Sea Rush**
Juncus squarrosus **Heath Rush**
Juncus subnodulosus
Blunt-flowered Rush
Juncus subulatus **Somerset Rush**
Luzula campestris **Field Wood-rush**
Luzula forsteri **Southern Wood-rush**
Luzula multiflora **Heath Wood-rush**
Luzula pilosa **Hairy Wood-rush**
Luzula sylvatica **Great Wood-rush**
Eriophorum angustifolium
Common Cottongrass
Trichophorum cespitosum **Deergrass**
Eleocharis palustris
Common Spike-rush
Bolboschoenus maritimus
Sea Club-rush
Scirpoides holoschoenus
Round-headed Club-rush
Isolepis cernua **Slender Club-rush**
Isolepis setacea **Bristle Club-rush**
Carex acutiformis **Lesser Pond-sedge**
Carex arenaria **Sand Sedge**
Carex binervis **Green-ribbed Sedge**
Carex caryophyllea **Spring-sedge**
Carex distans **Distant Sedge**
Carex disticha **Brown Sedge**
Carex divisa **Divided Sedge**
Carex divulsa **Grey Sedge**
Carex echinata **Star Sedge**
Carex extensa **Long-bracted Sedge**
Carex flacca **Glaucous Sedge**
Carex viridula **Common Yellow-sedge**
Carex flava **Large Yellow Sedge**
Carex hirta **Hairy Sedge**
Carex hostiana **Tawny Sedge**

Carex humilis **Dwarf Sedge**
Carex laevigata **Smooth-stalked Sedge**
Carex muricata **Prickly Sedge**
Carex nigra **Common Sedge**
Carex otrubae **False Fox-sedge**
Carex ovalis **Oval Sedge**
Carex panicea **Carnation Sedge**
Carex pendula **Pendulous Sedge**
Carex pilulifera **Pill Sedge**
Carex pulicaris **Flea Sedge**
Carex remota **Remote Sedge**
Carex riparia **Greater Pond-sedge**
Carex spicata **Spiked Sedge**
Carex sylvatica **Wood-sedge**
Nardus stricta **Mat-grass**
Milium effusum **Wood Millet**
Festuca arundinacea **Tall Fescue**
Festuca filiformis
Fine-leaved Sheep's-fescue
Festuca gigantea **Giant Fescue**
Festuca ovina **Sheep's-fescue**
Festuca pratensis **Meadow Fescue**
Festuca rubra **Red Fescue**
Lolium multiflorum **Italian Rye-grass**
Lolium perenne **Perennial Rye-grass**
Vulpia bromoides **Squirreltail Fescue**
Vulpia ciliata **Bearded Fescue**
Vulpia fasciculata **Dune Fescue**
Vulpia myuros **Rat's-tail Fescue**
Cynosurus cristatus **Crested Dog's-tail**
Puccinellia distans
Reflexed Saltmarsh-grass
Puccinellia maritima
Common Saltmarsh-grass
Briza maxima **Greater Quaking-grass**
Briza media **Quaking-grass**
Poa angustifolia
Narrow-leaved Meadow-grass
Poa annua **Annual Meadow-grass**
Poa bulbosa **Bulbous Meadow-grass**
Poa compressa
Flattened Meadow-grass
Poa humilis **Spreading Meadow-grass**
Poa nemoralis **Wood Meadow-grass**
Poa pratensis **Smooth Meadow-grass**
Poa trivialis **Rough Meadow-grass**
Dactylis glomerata **Cock's-foot**
Catapodium marinum **Sea Fern-grass**
Catapodium rigidum **Fern-grass**
Parapholis incurva **Curved Hard-grass**
Parapholis strigosa **Hard-grass**
Glyceria declinata **Small Sweet-grass**
Glyceria fluitans **Floating Sweet-grass**
Glyceria maxima **Reed Sweet-grass**
Glyceria notata **Plicate Sweet-grass**
Melica uniflora **Wood Melick**
Helictotrichon pratense
Meadow Oat-grass
Helictotrichon pubescens
Downy Oat-grass
Arrhenatherum elatius **False Oat-grass**
Avena fatua **Wild-oat**
Gaudinia fragilis **French Oat-grass**
Trisetum flavescens **Yellow Oat-grass**

Koeleria macrantha **Crested Hair-grass**
Koeleria vallesiana **Somerset Hair-grass**
Deschampsia cespitosa
Tufted Hair-grass
Deschampsia flexuosa **Wavy Hair-grass**
Holcus lanatus **Yorkshire-fog**
Holcus mollis **Creeping Soft-grass**
Aira caryophyllea **Silver Hair-grass**
Aira praecox **Early Hair-grass**
Anthoxanthum odoratum
Sweet Vernal-grass
Phalaris aquatica **Bulbous Canary-grass**
Phalaris arundinacea
Reed Canary-grass
Phalaris canariensis **Canary-grass**
Agrostis canina **Velvet Bent**
Agrostis capillaris **Common Bent**
Agrostis curtisii **Bristle Bent**
Agrostis gigantea **Black Bent**
Agrostis stolonifera **Creeping Bent**
Agrostis vinealis **Brown Bent**
Calamagrostis epigejos
Wood Small-reed
Ammophila arenaria **Marram**
Gastridium ventricosum **Nit-grass**
Lagurus ovatus **Hare's-tail**
Polypogon viridis **Water Bent**
Alopecurus bulbosus **Bulbous Foxtail**
Alopecurus geniculatus **Marsh Foxtail**
Alopecurus myosuroides **Black-grass**
Alopecurus pratensis **Meadow Foxtail**
Phleum arenarium **Sand Cat's-tail**
Phleum bertolonii **Smaller Cat's-tail**
Phleum pratense **Timothy**
Bromus commutatus **Meadow Brome**
Bromus hordeaceus **Soft-brome**
Bromus hordeaceus ssp. *ferronii*
Least Soft-brome
Bromus hordeaceus ssp. *thominei*
Sand Soft-brome
Bromus lepidus **Slender Soft-brome**
Bromus racemosus **Smooth Brome**
Bromus secalinus **Rye Brome**
Bromopsis erecta **Upright Brome**
Bromopsis inermis **Hungarian Brome**
Bromopsis ramosa **Hairy-brome**
Anisantha diandra **Great Brome**
Anisantha madritensis **Compact Brome**
Anisantha rigida **Ripgut Brome**
Anisantha sterilis **Barren Brome**
Anisantha tectorum **Drooping Brome**
Ceratochloa cathartica **Rescue Brome**
Brachypodium pinnatum
Heath False-brome
Brachypodium sylvaticum **False-brome**
Elymus caninus **Bearded Couch**
Elytrigia atherica **Sea Couch**
Elytrigia juncea **Sand Couch**
Elytrigia repens **Common Couch**
Leymus arenarius **Lyme Grass**
Hordeum distichon **Two-rowed Barley**
Hordeum jubatum **Foxtail Barley**
Hordeum marinum **Sea Barley**
Hordeum murinum **Wall Barley**

Hordeum secalinum **Meadow Barley**
Hordeum vulgare **Six-rowed Barley**
Danthonia decumbens **Heath-grass**
Molinia caerulea **Purple Moor-grass**
Phragmites australis **Common Reed**
Cynodon dactylon **Bermuda-grass**
Spartina anglica **Common Cord-grass**
Spartina maritima x *alterniflora* = *S.* x
townsendii **Townsend's Cord-grass**
Sparganium emersum
Unbranched Bur-reed
Sparganium erectum
Branched Bur-reed
Sparganium natans **Least Bur-reed**
Typha angustifolia **Lesser Bulrush**
Typha latifolia **Bulrush**
Ornithogalum angustifolium
Star of Bethlehem
Hyacinthoides hispanica
Spanish Bluebell
Hyacinthoides non-scripta **Bluebell**
Muscari armeniacum
Garden Grape-hyacinth
Allium ampeloprasum **Wild Leek**
Allium carinatum **Keeled Garlic**
Allium roseum **Rosy Garlic**
Allium triquetrum **Three-cornered Leek**
Allium ursinum **Ramsons**
Allium vineale **Wild Onion**
Leucojum aestivum **Summer Snowflake**
Galanthus nivalis **Snowdrop**
Narcissus pseudonarcissus **Daffodil**
Ruscus aculeatus **Butcher's Broom**
Iris foetidissima **Stinking Iris**
Iris germanica **Bearded Iris**
Iris pseudacorus **Yellow Iris**
Tamus communis **Black Bryony**
Epipactis palustris **Marsh Helleborine**
Neottia nidus-avis **Birdsnest Orchid**
Listera ovata **Common Twayblade**
Spiranthes spiralis
Autumn Lady's Tresses
Platanthera chlorantha
Greater Butterfly Orchid
Anacamptis pyramidalis
Pyramidal Orchid
Gymnadenia conopsea **Fragrant Orchid**
Dactylorhiza fuchsii
Common Spotted Orchid
Dactylorhiza maculata
Heath Spotted Orchid
Dactylorhiza praetermissa
Southern Marsh Orchid
Orchis mascula **Early Purple Orchid**
Orchis morio **Green-winged Orchid**
Himantoglossum hircinum **Lizard Orchid**
Ophrys apifera **Bee Orchid**
Ophrys insectifera **Fly Orchid**

APPENDIX 5
Marine invertebrates

Marine invertebrate that have been recorded on Somersets coast. Many species do not have common names.

MOLLUSCA
Single-shelled molluscs
Lepidochitona cinerea **Chiton**
Callochiton septemvalvis **Chiton**
Acanthochitona crinita **Chiton**
Emarginula fissura **Slit Limpet**
Diodora graeca **Keyhole Limpet**
Patella vulgata **Common Limpet**
Patella ulyssiponensis **China Limpet**
Patella depressa **Black-footed Limpet**
Tectura virginea
   White Tortoiseshell Limpet
Helcion pellucidum **Blue-rayed Limpet**
Gibbula cineraria **Grey Top Shell**
Gibbula umbilicalis **Flat Top Shell**
Calliostoma zizyphinum var. lyonsii
   Painted Top Shell
Osilinus lineatus **Toothed Top Shell**
Tricolia pullus **Pheasant Shell**
Lacuna pallidula **Pallid Chink Shell**
Lacuna parva **Least Chink Shell**
Lacuna vincta **Banded Chink Shell**
Littorina obtusata **Flat Periwinkle**
Littorina littorea **Common Periwinkle**
Littorina saxatilis **Rough Periwinkle**
Melarhaphe neritoides
   Small Periwinkle
Hydrobia ulvae **Laver Spire Shell**
Trivia arctica **Arctic Cowrie**
Trivia monacha **Spotted Cowrie**
Nucella lapillus **Dog Whelk**
Ocenebra erinacea **Sting Winkle**
Buccinum undatum **Common Whelk**
Hinia incrassata
   Thick-lipped Dog Whelk
Hinia reticulata **Netted Dog Whelk**

Sea slugs
Archidoris pseudoargus **Sea Lemon**
Aplysia punctata **Sea Hare**
Dendronotus frondosus **Sea slug**
Polycera faeroensis **Sea Slug**
Polycera quadrilineata **Sea Slug**
Berthella plumula **Yellow-plumed sea slug**

Bivalves
Nucula nucleus **Nut Shell**
Mytilus edulis **Common Mussel**
Musculus discors **Green Crenella**
Modiolus modiolus **Horse-mussel**
Anomia ephippium **Saddle Oyster**
Ostrea edulis **Common Oyster**
Chlamys varia **Variegated Scallop**
Aequipecten opercularis **Queen Scallop**
Cerastoderma edule **Common Cockle**

Venerupis senegalensis
   Pullet Carpet Shell
Scrobicularia plana
   Peppery Furrow Shell
Macoma balthica **Baltic Tellin**
Hiatella arctica **Wrinkled Rock Borer**
Spisula solida **Thick Trough Shell**
Timoclea ovata **Oval Venus**
Sphenia binghami **Small Gaper**

Cuttlefish and Octopus
Sepia officinalis **Common Cuttlefish**
Sepiola atlantica **Little Cuttle**
Octopus vulgaris **Common Octopus**
Eledone cirrhosa **Curled Octopus**

PORIFERA
Sponges
Axinella dissimilis
Ciocalypta penicillus
Cliona celata
Dysidea fragilis
Esperiopsis fucorum
Grantia compressa **Purse Sponge**
Halichondria panicea
   Breadcrumb Sponge
Haliclona oculata
Hemimycale columella
Hymeniacidon perleve
Hymeniacidon sanguinea
Polymastia boletiformis
Raspailia ramosa
Scypha ciliata
Stelligera stuposa
Suberites carnosus
Tethya aurantium
Pachymatisma johnstoni
Polymastia mammillaris
Dercitus bucklandi
Clathrina coriacea

ECHINODERMATA
Starfish and Urchins
Antedon bifida **Feather Star**
Asterias rubens **Common Starfish**
Asterina gibbosa
Crossaster papposus **Common Sun Star**

Cucumariidae
Henricia oculata
Marthasterias glacialis
Ophiocomina nigra
Ophiothrix fragilis **Common Brittlestar**
Ophiura ophiura **Brittlestar**
Echinus esculentus **Edible Sea Urchin**

CRUSTACEA
Shrimps, Crabs and Barnacles
Ligia oceanica **Common Sea Slater**
Orchestia gammarellus **Sand Hopper**
Astacilla longicornis
Semibalanus balanoides
   an Acorn Barnacle
Balanus balanus **an Acorn Barnacle**
Balanus crenatus **an Acorn Barnacle**
Balanus improvisus **an Acorn Barnacle**
Balanus perforatus **an Acorn Barnacle**
Chthamalus montagui
   Montagu's Stellate Barnacle
Chthamalus stellatus
   Poli's Stellate Barnacle
Elminius modestus **an Acorn Barnacle**
Verruca stroemia **Wart Barnacle**
Cancer pagurus **Edible Crab**
Carcinus maenas **Green Shore Crab**
Hyas araneus **Great Spider Crab**
Munida rugosa **Rugose Squat Lobster**
Necora puber **Velvet Swimming Crab**
Pagurus bernhardus **a Hermit crab**
Pagurus prideaux **a Hermit crab**
Pisidia longicornis
   Long-clawed Porcelain Crab
Porcellana platycheles
   Broad-clawed Porcelain Crab
Homarus gammarus **Common Lobster**
Maja squinado **Common Spider Crab**
Crangon crangon **Brown Shrimp**
Palaemon elegans
Palaemon serratus **Common Prawn**

CNIDARIA
Sea Firs
Abietinaria abietina
Amphisbetia operculata
Halecium halecinum
Hydrallmania falcata
Kirchenpaueria pinnata
Nemertesia antennina **Sea Beard**
Nemertesia ramosa
Obelia dichotoma
Obelia geniculata
Plumularia setacea
Sertularia argentea
Sertularia cupressina **Whiteweed**
Tridentata distans
Tubularia indivisa

Jellyfish
Aurelia aurita **Moon Jellyfish**
Chrysaora hysoscella
   Compass Jellyfish

Chiton, a 2 cm long mollusc

Common Periwinkle

Common Cockle

Breadcrumb Sponge

Young Edible Crab

Sea Anemones
Actinia equina **Beadlet Anemone**
Actinia fragacea **Strawberry Anemone**
Actinothoe sphyrodeta
  Sandalled Anemone
Alcyonium digitatum
Anemonia viridis **Snakelocks Anemone**
Cereus pedunculatus **Daisy Anemone**
Halecium halecinum
Urticina felina **Dahlia Anemone**
Nemertesia antennina
Nemertesia ramosa
Epizoanthus couchii
Adamsia carciniopados **Cloak Anemone**
Aulactinia verrucosa **Gem Anemone**
Stomphia coccinea

BRYOZOA Sea Mats
Aetea anquina **Snakes Head Coralline**
Electra pilosa
Electra monostachys
Electra crustulenta
Alcyonidium diaphanum
Alcyonidium hirsutum
Alcyonidium mytili
Bicellariella ciliata

Bugula flabellata
Bugula plumosa
Bugula turbinata
Callopora lineata
Cellaria sinuosa
Cellaria fistulosa
Crisia eburnea
Diplosolen obelia
Disporella hispida
Escharella immersa **Hornwrack**
Flustra foliacea
Flustrellidra hispida
Phaeostachys spinifera
Plagioecia patina
Schizomavella auriculata
Schizomavella linearis
Smittoidea reticulata
Umbonula littoralis
Vesicularia spinosa
Porella compressa
Membranipora membranacea **Sea Mat**

ANNELIDAE Marine Worms
Nereis diversicolor **Estuary Ragworm**
Nereis virens **King Ragworm**
Arenicola marina **Blow Lugworm**

Bispira volutacornis
Eulalia viridis **Greenleaf Worm**
Filograna implexa
Hydroides norvegica
Lanice conchilega **Sand Mason Worm**
Perinereis cultrifera **Ragworm**
Pomatoceros triqueter
Pseudopotamilla reniformis
Spirobis corallinae
Spirorbis rupestris
Sabella pavonina **Peacock Worm**
Sabellaria spinulosa
Sabellaria alveolata **Honeycomb Worm**

UROCHORDATA Sea Squirts
Ascidia mentula
Botryllus schlosseri **Star Ascidian**
Clavelina lepadiformis
  Light Bulb Seasquirt
Dendrodoa grossularia
Polycarpa pomaria
Pycnoclavella aurilucens
  Orange Lights Seasquirt
Aplidium punctum

Sea Mat

Honeycomb Worm

APPENDIX 6
Insects

Dragonflies and damselflies, grasshoppers and crickets, and butterflies seen regularly along Somerset's coast

DRAGONFLIES & DAMSELFLIES
Calopteryx virgo **Beautiful Demoiselle**
Calopteryx splendens
   Banded Demoiselle
Lestes sponsa **Emerald Damselfly**
Pyrrhosoma nymphula
   Large Red Damselfly
Coenagrion puella **Azure Damselfly**
Enallagma cyathigerum
   Common Blue Damselfly
Ischnura elegans **Blue-tailed Damselfly**
Brachytron pratense **Hairy Dragonfly**
Aeshna juncea **Common Hawker**
Aeshna mixta **Migrant Hawker**
Aeshna cyanea **Southern Hawker**
Aeshna grandis **Brown Hawker**
Anax imperator **Emperor Dragonfly**
Cordulegaster boltonii
   Golden-ringed Dragonfly
Libellula quadrimaculata
   Four-spotted Chaser
Libellula depressa **Broad-bodied Chaser**
Orthetrum cancellatum
   Black-tailed Skimmer
Orthetrum coerulescens
   Keeled Skimmer
Sympetrum striolatum **Common Darter**
Sympetrum sanguineum **Ruddy Darter**
Sympetrum danae **Black Darter**
Sympetrum flaveolum
   Yellow-winged Darter
Sympetrum fonscolombii
   Red-veined Darter

GRASSHOPPERS & CRICKETS
Meconema thalassinum
   Oak Bush-cricket
Tettigonia viridissima
   Great Green Bush-cricket
Pholidoptera griseoaptera
   Dark Bush-cricket
Platycleis albopunctata
   Grey Bush-cricket
Conocephalus dorsalis
   Short-winged Cone-head
Leptophyes punctatissima
   Speckled Bush-cricket
Tetrix subulata **Slender Groundhopper**
Tetrix undulata **Common Groundhopper**
Stenobothrus lineatus
   Stripe-winged Grasshopper
Omocestus rufipes
   Woodland Grasshopper
Omocestus viridulus
   Common Green Grasshopper
Chorthippus brunneus
   Field Grasshopper
Chorthippus parallelus
   Meadow Grasshopper
Chorthippus albomarginatus
   Lesser Marsh Grasshopper
Gomphocerippus rufus
   Rufous Grasshopper
Myrmeleotettix maculatus
   Mottled Grasshopper

BUTTERFLIES
Thymelicus sylvestris **Small Skipper**
Thymelicus lineola **Essex Skipper**
Ochlodes faunus **Large Skipper**
Erynnis tages **Dingy Skipper**
Pyrgus malvae **Grizzled Skipper**
Colias croceus **Clouded Yellow**
Gonepteryx rhamni **Brimstone**
Pieris brassicae **Large White**
Pieris rapae **Small White**
Pieris napi **Green-veined White**
Anthocharis cardamines **Orange-tip**
Callophrys rubi **Green Hairstreak**
Neozephyrus quercus **Purple Hairstreak**
Lycaena phlaeas **Small Copper**
Cupido minimus **Small Blue**
Aricia agestis **Brown Argus**
Polyommatus icarus **Common Blue**
Lysandra coridon **Chalkhill Blue**
Celastrina argiolus **Holly Blue**
Vanessa atalanta **Red Admiral**
Vanessa cardui **Painted Lady**
Aglais urticae **Small Tortoiseshell**
Inachis io **Peacock**
Polygonia c-album **Comma**
Boloria selene
   Small Pearl-bordered Fritillary
Argynnis aglaja **Dark Green Fritillary**
Argynnis paphia
   Silver-washed Fritillary
Melitaea athalia **Heath Fritillary**
Pararge aegeria **Speckled Wood**
Lasiommata megera **Wall**
Melanargia galathea **Marbled White**
Hipparchia semele **Grayling**
Pyronia tithonus **Gatekeeper**
Maniola jurtina **Meadow Brown**
Aphantopus hyperantus **Ringlet**
Coenonympha pamphilus **Small Heath**

Golden-ringed Dragonfly

Field Grasshopper

Grizzled Skipper

Small Copper

APPENDIX 7
Birds

This list covers birds that nest on or very close to the coast or that visit the coast on a regular basis during the year or in the spring autumn and winter migration period. It is not a complete list of every bird that has been seen on Somersets coast. Breeding birds are indicated as: ■ breeds roughly within 500 metres of the coast; ■ breeds in Somerset.

- ■ *Tachybaptus ruficollis* **Little Grebe**
- ■ *Podiceps cristatus*
  Great Crested Grebe
- ■ *Fulmarus glacialis* **Fulmar**
- *Puffinus puffinus* **Manx Shearwater**
- *Hydrobates pelagicus* **Storm Petrel**
- *Morus bassanus* **Gannet**
- ■ *Phalacrocorax carbo* **Cormorant**
- *Phalacrocorax aristotelis* **Shag**
- ■ *Egretta garzetta* **Little Egret**
- ■ *Ardea cinerea* **Grey Heron**
- ■ *Botaurus stellaris* **Bittern**
- ■ *Cygnus olor* **Mute Swan**
- *Cygnus columbianus* **Bewick's Swan**
- ■ *Branta canadensis* **Canada Goose**
- *Branta bernicla bernicula*
  Dark-bellied Brent Goose
- *Branta bernicla hrota*
  Light-bellied Brent Goose
- ■ *Tadorna tadorna* **Shelduck**
- ■ *Anas platyrhynchos* **Mallard**
- *Anas acuta* **Pintail**
- ■ *Anas clypeata* **Shoveler**
- *Anas penelope* **Wigeon**
- ■ *Anas crecca* **Teal**
- *Aythya marila* **Greater Scaup**
- *Melanitta nigra* **Common Scoter**
- ■ *Mergus merganser* **Goosander**
- *Mergus serrator*
  Red-breasted Merganser
- *Gavia stellata* **Red Throated Diver**
- *Gavia arctica* **Black Throated Diver**
- *Gavia immer* **Great Northern Diver**
- ■ *Circus aeruginosus* **Marsh Harrier**
- ■ *Buteo buteo* **Common Buzzard**
- ■ *Accipiter nisus* **Sparrowhawk**
- ■ *Falco tinnunculus* **Kestrel**
- ■ *Falco subbuteo* **Hobby**
- ■ *Falco peregrinus* **Peregrine Falcon**
- ■ *Falco columbarius* **Merlin**
- ■ *Rallus aquaticus* **Water Rail**
- ■ *Gallinula chloropus* **Moorhen**
- ■ *Fulica atra* **Coot**
- *Grus grus* **Crane**
- ■ *Haematopus ostralegus* **Oystercatcher**
- *Recurvirostra avosetta* **Avocet**
- ■ *Charadrius hiaticula* **Ringed Plover**

- *Pluvialis squatarola* **Grey Plover**
- *Pluvialis apricaria* **Golden Plover**
- ■ *Vanellus vanellus* **Lapwing**
- *Calidris canutus* **Knot**
- *Calidris alba* **Sanderling**
- *Calidris alpina* **Dunlin**
- *Calidris minuta* **Little Stint**
- *Calidris maritima* **Purple Sandpiper**
- *Actitis hypoleucos* **Common Sandpiper**
- ■ *Tringa totanus* **Redshank**
- *Tringa erythropus* **Spotted Redshank**
- *Tringa ochropus* **Green Sandpiper**
- *Tringa nebularia* **Greenshank**
- *Arenaria interpres* **Turnstone**
- *Limosa limosa* **Black-tailed Godwit**
- *Limosa lapponica* **Bar-tailed Godwit**
- ■ *Numenius arquata* **Curlew**
- *Numenius phaeopus* **Whimbrel**
- ■ *Scolopax rusticola* **Woodcock**
- ■ *Gallinago gallinago* **Snipe**
- *Lymnocryptes minimus* **Jack Snipe**
- *Stercorarius skua* **Great Skua**
- *Stercorarius parasiticus* **Arctic Skua**
- *Rissa tridactyla* **Kittiwake**
- ■ *Larus ridibundus* **Black-headed Gull**
- *Larus melanocephalus*
  Mediteranean Gull
- *Larus canus* **Common Gull**
- ■ *Larus argentatus* **Herring Gull**
- ■ *Larus fuscus* **Lesser Black-backed Gull**
- ■ *Larus marinus* **Great Black-backed Gull**
- ■ *Sterna hirundo* **Common Tern**
- *Sterna paradisaea* **Arctic Tern**
- *Uria aalge* **Guillemot**
- *Alca torda* **Razorbill**
- ■ *Columba oenas* **Stock Dove**
- ■ *Columba palumbus* **Wood Pigeon**
- ■ *Streptopelia decaocto* **Collared Dove**
- ■ *Streptopelia turtur* **Turtle Dove**
- ■ *Cuculus canorus* **Common Cuckoo**
- ■ *Strix aluco* **Tawny Owl**
- ■ *Asio otus* **Long-eared Owl**
- *Asio flammeus* **Short-eared Owl**
- ■ *Athene noctua* **Little Owl**
- ■ *Tyto alba* **Barn Owl**
- ■ *Caprimulgus europaeus* **Nightjar**
- ■ *Apus apus* **Common Swift**

- ■ *Alcedo atthis* **Kingfisher**
- ■ *Picus viridis* **Green Woodpecker**
- ■ *Dendrocopos major*
  Great Spotted Woodpecker
- ■ *Dendrocopos minor*
  Lesser Spotted Woodpecker
- ■ *Alauda arvensis* **Skylark**
- ■ *Riparia riparia* **Sand Martin**
- ■ *Delichon urbicum* **House Martin**
- ■ *Hirundo rustica* **Swallow**
- ■ *Anthus pratensis* **Meadow Pipit**
- ■ *Anthus trivialis* **Tree Pipit**
- ■ *Anthus petrosus* **Rock Pipit**
- *Anthus spinoletta* **Water Pipit**
- ■ *Motacilla alba* **Pied Wagtail**
- ■ *Motacilla cinerea* **Grey Wagtail**
- ■ *Motacilla flava* **Yellow Wagtail**
- ■ *Troglodytes troglodytes* **Wren**
- ■ *Cinclus cinclus* **Dipper**
- ■ *Prunella modularis* **Dunnock**
- ■ *Erithacus rubecula* **Robin**
- ■ *Luscinia magarhynchos* **Nightingale**
- ■ *Phoenicurus phoenicurus* **Redstart**
- *Phoenicurus ochruros* **Black Redstart**
- ■ *Oenanthe oenanthe* **Wheatear**
- ■ *Saxicola rubetra* **Whinchat**
- ■ *Saxicola torquata* **Stonechat**
- ■ *Turdus philomelos* **Song Thrush**
- *Turdus iliacus* **Redwing**
- ■ *Turdus viscivorus* **Mistle Thrush**
- *Turdus pilaris* **Fieldfare**
- ■ *Turdus merula* **Blackbird**
- *Turdus torquatus* **Ring Ouzel**
- ■ *Sylvia borin* **Garden Warbler**
- ■ *Sylvia atricapilla* **Blackcap**
- ■ *Sylvia curruca* **Lesser Whitethroat**
- ■ *Sylvia communis* **Whitethroat**
- ■ *Sylvia undata* **Dartford Warbler**
- ■ *Acrocephalus schoenobaenus*
  Sedge Warbler
- ■ *Acrocephalus scirpaceus*
  Reed Warbler
- ■ *Locustella naevia*
  Grasshopper Warbler
- ■ *Cettia cetti* **Cetti's Warbler**
- ■ *Phylloscopus trochilus*
  Willow Warbler

Common Buzzard

Common Sandpiper

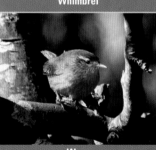

Whimbrel

Wren

Wheatear